WOW!
WOOL-ON-WOOL
FoLK-ART QUILTS

Revised and Expanded Edition

JANET CARIJA BRANDT

Martingale®
& COMPANY

That Patchwork Place® is an imprint of Martingale & Company®.

WOW! Wool-on-Wool Folk-Art Quilts,
Revised and Expanded Edition
© 2004 by Janet Carija Brandt

Martingale & Company
20205 144th Avenue NE
Woodinville, WA 98072-8478 USA
www.martingale-pub.com

Printed in China
09 08 07 06 05 04   8 7 6 5 4 3 2 1

Library of Congress Cataloging-in-Publication Data

Brandt, Janet Carija.
    WOW! : wool-on-wool folk-art quilts / Janet Carija Brandt.
Rev. and expanded ed.
        p. cm.
    Rev. ed. of: Wool-on-wool folk-art quilts. Bothell, WA : That Patchwork Place, c1995.
    Includes bibliographical references.
    ISBN 1-56477-591-7
    1. Quilting—Patterns. 2. Appliqué—Patterns. 3. Wool quilts.
4. Rugs, Hooked. I. Title: Wool-on-wool folk-art quilts. II. Brandt, Janet Carija. Wool-on-wool folk-art quilts. III. Title.
    TT835.B66 2004
    746.46'041—dc22
                                                    2004014853

MISSION STATEMENT

Dedicated to providing quality products
and service to inspire creativity.

CREDITS

President • NANCY J. MARTIN
CEO • DANIEL J. MARTIN
Publisher • JANE HAMADA
Editorial Director • MARY V. GREEN
Managing Editor • TINA COOK
Technical Editor • ELLEN PAHL
Copy Editor • ELLEN BALSTAD
Design Director • STAN GREEN
Illustrator • LAUREL STRAND
Text Designer • TRINA STAHL
Cover Designer • STAN GREEN
Photographer • BRENT KANE

DEDICATION

To Chris, who makes my creative life possible

ACKNOWLEDGMENTS

A big thank-you to all the wonderful people at Martingale & Company, past and present, who had the foresight 10 years ago to showcase my work, and who have the enthusiasm today to present it revised, expanded, and updated! Thank you to Mary Green and Karen Costello Soltys for steering it through the publishing process. And thank you to Ellen Pahl and Ellen Balstad for meticulous and thoughtful editing.

CONTENTS

PREFACE

In 1994, when I found out That Patchwork Place wanted to publish *WOW! Wool-On-Wool Folk-Art Quilts,* I was thrilled. Now 10 years later, I am equally delighted that I have the pleasure of bringing you this revised edition. What a difference 10 years makes! When the book was first released, most quilt stores didn't carry so much as a scrap of wool. And the Internet was in its infancy, which meant that it was not a viable source for wool. That left thrift stores for recycled wool or the occasional garment fabric store where the salespeople didn't know what to make of us. "You want to machine wash and dry the wool!? You'll ruin it!" they cried. But we didn't ruin it, we felted it. And we had wonderful fun in the process. Slowly the look caught on.

Wool is still my favorite fabric to stitch on, but whether you choose wool, cotton, or felt, I hope you'll enjoy these projects.

INTRODUCTION

My relationship with textiles started at an early age. When I was a preteen and teenager, my parents owned a beautiful dress shop. I did small interior store displays and eventually changed the window displays each week. During my junior year of high school, I got a job drawing the weekly fashion illustration for the Sunday paper, which I continued even when I went away to college. Looking back, I am amazed and thankful for the responsibilities I was given at such an early age.

In college, I earned a degree in architecture, but I eventually returned to textiles in 1986 when I hooked my first rug. From there I began designing my own rug-hooking patterns, and in 1990 I started Carijarts, a mail-order catalog of rug-hooking patterns and kits. I have written many articles for *Rug Hooking* magazine, and I was named among the top 200 craftsmen by *Early American Life* magazine each of the years that I submitted work. Quite simply, I love to design things, whether they are built, sewn, or hooked.

I've tinkered with fabric for as long as I can remember. A couple of years before writing the first edition of *WOW!*, I was hooking a rug and thinking there must be a more timely way to get the ideas out of my head and into the fabric. I had notebooks filled with ideas, shelves loaded with wool, and dye pots simmering on the stove. Then I thought, why not combine the luscious textures and colors of wool as they appear in hooked

rugs with the techniques of appliqué and quilting? That was the beginning of *Wool-on-Wool Folk-Art Quilts.*

My designs are pure whimsy. I like to create pieces that you won't see anywhere else. After all,

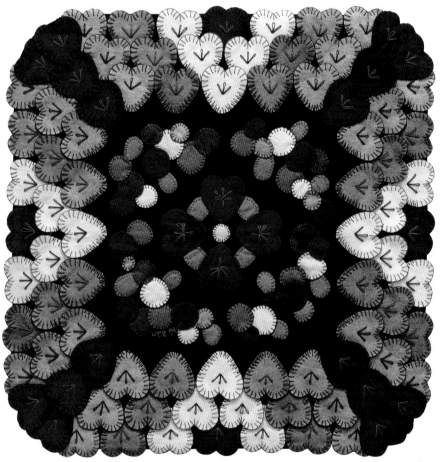

isn't that why we spend the time making something ourselves? "See, I made this!" we sometimes want to shout when we finish a project.

This is a book to inspire and guide you, to kindle your creative spirit. It is a chance to play with color, to perhaps play with a fabric you haven't used before, and to tinker anew.

ALL ABOUT WOOL

THE BASIC ingredient for a beautiful wool appliqué quilt or rug is quite simply, wool. Your quilt or rug can be made completely from all new wool, all old wool, or a combination of both. Here are a few guidelines for starting your wool stockpile.

SELECTING NEW WOOL

Shopping for new wool used to be a challenge. When I originally wrote this book in 1994, the biggest obstacle for someone interested in wool appliqué or rug hooking was knowing where to find wool. Not anymore! Chances are excellent that your local quilt shop now has a beautiful assortment of wools to choose from. If they don't have it, I'm sure they can recommend someone who does.

The ideal wool is a tightly woven, 100% medium-weight wool, which is often used to make skirts and dresses. After being machine washed and dried, woven wool will not unravel easily along the edge. You are not as limited in your wool choices for wool appliqué as you are for rug hooking. Some wool is too heavy or too loosely woven to hook with but will

still work for appliqué. Tight or loose weave; heavyweight or lightweight; plain weave or twill; solids or plaids, stripes, and checks—all of these can be good options for wool appliqué, so how do you choose?

Let's start with the first set of choices: tight weave or loose weave. Of all the choices, this is the one about which I am most particular. The tighter the weave, the easier it is to work with. If the fabric is 100% wool, even a very loose weave might be made usable by shrinking it, which is also called felting. Wool is felted when it is run through hot and cold water cycles in the washing machine. See "Washing and Drying Wool" on page 7. If you love the color and weight of a loosely woven piece of wool, but shrinking doesn't work and you want to use it "no matter what," space your blanket stitches a little closer together for an appliqué project or cut your wool strips a little wider for a rug-hooking project.

When faced with all the various weights of wool fabric, look for mediumweight wool. However, don't pass up other weights if the color, weave, and fiber content are right. Lightweight wool makes a wonderful background fabric but only when equally lightweight fabric is used for the appliqués. A heavyweight wool, on the other hand, can support light, medium, or heavyweight appliqués. For rug hooking, cut lightweight wool strips a little wider than what is normal for your rug and cut heavier wool a little narrower than normal. See "Cutting Strips" on page 25.

Twills and tweeds are more difficult to work with than plain weaves, but what goodies you pass by if you don't at least try to use them! The solution here is the same as it was for loosely woven wool; try to shrink the fabric. If you are successful, all the stray threads won't present problems, and you'll greatly increase your palette of color and texture. As for the question of using solids or plaids, stripes, and checks, I love and use them all.

RECYCLING WOOL CLOTHING

Collecting old wool clothing to recycle into new wool appliqué projects and rug hooking is great fun. Your neighbor's garage sale or your own closets are perfect places to begin your hunt. Thrift shops such as the Salvation Army or Goodwill are a wool picker's paradise. Enlist the help of friends who love to shop and hunt for bargains.

As you do for new wool, look for fabric that is 100% wool. A skirt-weight wool or a wool flannel with a tight weave is great. Of course, there are exceptions here too. If I find a skirt in an absolutely luscious color, and the weight and weave are right but the fiber content label says it is not 100% wool, I might still go for it. I will go as low as 80% wool if it is perfect to use as it is; otherwise, I will not bother with it. There are two reasons for this. First, if the weave is not tight enough originally, no amount of washing and drying of a fabric blend will shrink it. Second, if I do want to change the color, a fabric blend will not take the dye as predictably or as evenly as 100%-wool fabric. It just is not worth the trouble.

A 100%-wool fabric takes up the dye more intensely than a wool blend. The plaids on the left are wool blends. The solid colors on the right are 100% wool.

I usually choose from the skirt rack when I shop. Slacks and jackets are too much work to take apart, and you're left with only small pieces for all your effort. As with new wool, select solid colors, plaids, stripes, checks, and even tweeds. Wool appliqué and rug-hooking projects can incorporate any pattern and texture.

As soon as I get home with my wool treasures, I sort the skirts by color, and then I machine wash and dry them. See "Washing and Drying Wool" below. This serves three purposes. First, I now know I am working with clean fabric; second, the wools are now mothproof (moths love dirt, not wool); and third, the wool has probably shrunk slightly (felted) and is nice and soft. This makes the wool easier to work with.

Next, I cut off the waistbands and save the buttons. Many people save the zippers and the labels. I have seen some wonderful shirts and jackets with labels appliquéd all over them, but my thriftiness only extends to the buttons. Last of all, I rip out the seams and hems, and then I step back and admire the soft, cuddly pile of wool.

WASHING AND DRYING WOOL

It is important to wash even new wool to shrink or felt it before you use it. For the purposes of wool appliqué and hooked rugs, felted wool is any wool that has shrunk or become slightly matted so that it does not easily unravel. This is usually achieved by simply machine washing and drying.

I throw the wool in the washing machine with a little detergent and the machine set on the warm and gentle cycle. I use regular laundry detergent with no bleach additives, and I add ¼ cup for a full load—less for a partial load. If I want the fabric to be highly felted, I set the washing machine on the hot wash/cold rinse and normal cycle. I wash the wool at this setting, and sometimes repeat if necessary, until I am satisfied with the results. Then I dry the wool on a medium dryer setting until it is completely dry and fluffy.

DYEING WOOL

PLEASE DON'T skip this section. So many people are frightened by the idea of dyeing, but it is easy and great fun! The biggest myth about dyeing is "It's so messy!" This is not necessarily true. Before I started dyeing, I had a very white kitchen. After dyeing a large volume of wool, I still have a very white kitchen, and I can assure you this has nothing to do with any great housekeeping skills!

DYEING SUPPLIES AND EQUIPMENT

Keep all dyeing equipment separate from household cooking utensils and pans. Do not use any dyeing equipment for cooking. Most supplies are readily available. For dyes and other specialty items, see "Resources and Inspiration" on page 111. You will need the following:

- One or more white enamel pans, 5-quart size or larger. White pans work best, allowing you to see the color better than dark pans do. Use large pots for dyeing large pieces of wool. If the wool is too tightly packed in the dye pot, the resulting color will be uneven (but interesting).
- A large mixing spoon and tongs (Use any type of utensil except galvanized metal.)
- Aluminum foil for spot dyeing
- Pyrex pan (approximately 11" x 13") for spot dyeing
- Heavy rubber gloves
- Dust mask
- White vinegar (I buy it by the gallon.)
- Dyes (I use Cushing Perfection dyes.)
- Small measuring cups
- Small measuring spoons
- Triple Over Dye (TOD) measuring spoon (This is a special measuring spoon with a ¹⁄₃₂ teaspoon on one end and a ¼ teaspoon on the other. It is optional but very handy.)

Dyeing equipment: enamel pot, spoon, tongs, dyes, measuring cups and spoons, white vinegar, and TOD measuring spoon

BASIC DYEING METHOD

If you plan to work in your kitchen, move or cover all food-related items before beginning the dyeing process. Cover the counters with newspaper as well. Work in a well-ventilated area, and wear your gloves and dust mask at all times. The dyes are superfine powders that are easily inhaled if you do not take precautions.

1. At least one hour before dyeing, presoak all wool in lukewarm water with just a few drops of liquid soap. This soaking moistens the fibers so that they will take up the dye evenly. Sometimes I toss the wool into a tub of water the night before so that I know it has had plenty of time to soak. Note that the soap is rinsed out later when I rinse out the vinegar and excess dye at the end of the process.

2. Fill an enamel pan about ¾ full of water. Bring to a boil.

3. Carefully measure your dyes into a small glass, plastic cup, or pan, and then add ½ cup or so of boiling water to dissolve the dye. In this dyeing procedure, the amount of water is not important. The water just serves as a way of carrying the dye to the wool. The amount of dye in proportion to the amount of wool is what determines the final color.

4. After all of the dye is dissolved (there should be no more specks floating in the water), pour the solution into the large enamel pan of boiling water. Stir well.

5. Now add the wool, stirring often.

6. After about five minutes, add ½ cup of white vinegar to the dye pot. This helps the wool take up and keep the dye. Keep stirring gently. The more often you stir, the more even your color will be. Keep the water at a slow simmer.

7. Simmer the wool until all the dye is absorbed into the fabric and the water is clear, or until the desired color is reached. Remember, wet wool in the dye pot looks much darker than it will look when it is dry.

8. Remove the wool with tongs and place it in a tray or shallow pan to transport it to the sink. Rinse gently, first in hot water, and then in gradually cooler water.

9. Hang or machine dry.

Now that wasn't so bad, was it? From this basic procedure, you can create all kinds of wonderful colors and effects. In addition to this, there is dip dyeing, spot dyeing, gradation dyeing, transitional dyeing, or the easiest of all, random dyeing.

DIP DYEING

For dip dyeing, start with a well-soaked piece of wool (see step 1 of "Basic Dyeing Method" at left) that measures approximately 11" x 14". To a large enamel pan of boiling water, add dye that has already been dissolved in a small amount of boiling water. Remember, it isn't the amount of water that determines the color; it is the proportion of dye to fabric.

Add ¼ cup of white vinegar to the dye pot and stir well. Wearing heavy rubber gloves (to protect your fingers from the steam and boiling water), dip one of the short ends of the wool into the dye pot.

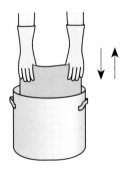

Keep the wool moving, dipping it in an up-and-down motion so that a solid line does not appear between the natural color of the wool and the dyed area. The lower edge of the wool (the edge in the dye pot) will become a nice, bright color fading into the natural color of the wool. If you wish, give the entire piece of wool one quick dip into the dyebath so that a very subtle wash of color extends to the top edge. When all of the dye has been taken up by the wool, or when you have obtained the color you want, set the wool aside.

In a fresh pan of boiling water, add another color of dye that has been dissolved in a small amount (¼ cup) of boiling water. Add ¼ cup of white vinegar to the boiling water and dye mixture.

Now repeat the dipping procedure, this time putting the opposite end of the wool into the dye pot. Gently dip the wool in an up-and-down motion until the color is bright on the bottom and blends and mixes with the color on top.

Remember to always keep the wool gently moving up and down so that a solid line of dye does not appear in the middle of your wool. When you have the color you want (keep in mind that wet wool is much darker than dry wool), or all of the dye is taken up from the dye pot, rinse the wool in hot, and then warm, and finally cool water to remove the soap and vinegar. Line or machine dry.

GRADATION DYEING

This method produces several pieces of wool that are each slightly darker than the next, but all the pieces are the same color. Prepare several dyebaths with the same color of dye, but for each dyebath add a slightly stronger concentration of dye. For example, you might try adding ¹⁄₃₂ teaspoon of dye for the first dyebath, ¹⁄₁₆ teaspoon for the second, ³⁄₃₂ teaspoon for the third, and ⅛ teaspoon for the fourth. Dye one piece of wool per dyebath. Refer to "Basic Dyeing Method" on page 9 for preparation and dyeing basics.

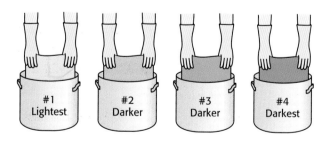

TRANSITIONAL DYEING

This method involves dyeing several pieces of wool and changing the dye from one color to another; for example, changing from pink to purple. In our example, the first dyebath would contain only pink dye, so the piece of wool dyed in it would be pure pink. For the second dyebath, you would use the same total amount of dye but a little less pink and a small amount of purple. The resulting pink piece would have just a tiny hint of purple. If the third dyebath contained equal amounts of pink and purple dye, and the fourth dyebath contained the reverse amounts of dye as the second dyebath, the resulting pieces would be more and more purple. If you dye the last piece in a pure purple dyebath, you will have a gradation of wool pieces from one hue to the next. You can have any number of swatches of wool, any ratio, and any combination of dye colors. Experiment to achieve even gradations of colors. Remember to add vinegar to the dyebaths to fix the color, and refer to "Basic Dyeing Method" on page 9 for preparation and dyeing basics.

SPOT DYEING

Spot dyeing gives unusual, unpredictable, but always fun results. Due to the varying concentrations and different colors of dye in different areas of a single piece of wool, you will obtain light and dark areas as well as several colors within the same piece.

1. Presoak the wool in water and vinegar. Use ½ cup of vinegar for every ½ yard of wool.

2. Line the bottom of a shallow Pyrex baking dish with crumpled aluminum foil. Place crumpled wet wool on top of the foil. Keep the wool in a single, but not smooth, layer.

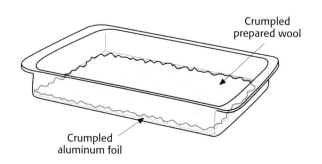

3. Dissolve each color of dye in approximately ¼ cup of boiling water. For each piece of wool, I find that a total of two or three different colors usually works best.

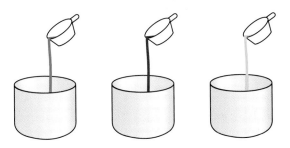

4. Spoon small amounts of each dye color over the wool in a random pattern.

5. Carefully add just enough boiling water at the edge of the wool to keep the wool moist but not swimming in lots of water. Too much water will make the colors run together and turn muddy; not enough will cause the wool to dry out and possibly burn when you steam it in the oven (see step 6).

6. Cover the pan with foil and steam the wool in the oven for 30 minutes at 250°F. Check occasionally to make sure the wool has not dried out. Cool, rinse, and dry.

RANDOM DYEING

For this method, include pieces of several different wools (an assortment of colors, patterns, and/or textures) in the same dyebath. The reason for doing this is similar to the reason quilters tea-dye fabrics. All of the resulting colors will work together, whether they are soft and pastel or strong and dark.

Random dyeing works best when making a pictorial-type hooked rug, such as "Red Hen Rug" on page 98. By using eight different recycled wools and five different dye-color combinations, I came up with over forty colors of wool to use for hooking the rug. In a nonsymmetrical rug of this type, the colors do not need to match perfectly from one side of the rug to the other.

When working on an Asian-style or a symmetrical design, carefully measure the wool and the dye so that you can create the same color again if you run out of wool. Keeping notes and records as you work provides valuable backup information later.

1. Begin by tearing your wool into pieces that are easy to handle. If you rip or tear your wool, you will get perfectly straight edges. You will also know where the grain line is.

2. If you are dyeing a piece of wool for the background of a specific quilt, tear the wool the size of the finished piece plus a couple of inches for shrinkage.

3. Prepare and dye the wool following the steps in "Basic Dyeing Method" on page 9. After

Dyeing transforms dull recycled wools into a rainbow of new shades.

rinsing and gently squeezing the water out of the wool, you will have a pretty good idea of the final color. Do you want lighter tints? Either add more wool or less dye next time. Do you want darker shades? Either add less wool or more dye.

Keep in mind that the original color of the wool will also make a difference in the final color. Light colors show the dye more readily than dark colors.

See how simple it is? You can of course experiment with any color combination you like. You really cannot make a mistake. The color that you think is ugly today may be the exact shade you are looking for tomorrow.

TWO FOR ONE

If you like the color of your wool before the water is clear, you can remove the wool after you have added the vinegar. Keep in mind that the wool looks darker when it is wet. Toss another piece of presoaked wool into the remaining dye, add a little more vinegar (¼ cup), and simmer until clear. This second batch probably will not be as dark as the first but will coordinate perfectly and can be used to great advantage in shading different designs.

APPLIQUÉ AND QUILTING TECHNIQUES

IF YOU'VE never worked with wool before, you're in for a treat. It feels wonderful and comes in gorgeous colors, whether you dye your own or purchase it. It's easy to stitch and soothing to a stitcher's soul.

TOOLS AND SUPPLIES

For making the wool appliqué projects, you will need the following supplies:

- 1"-long dressmaker pins
- Sequin pins (½"-long pins found in craft-supply stores)
- Tracing paper
- Plastic template sheets (frosted so that you can see it; available at quilt shops)
- Lightweight, nonfusible interfacing
- Chalk pencils
- Scissors (one pair for fabric and one for paper; small scissors are handy for details)
- Embroidery floss or perle cotton
- Basting thread (regular, all-purpose sewing thread is fine)
- Needles (use whatever works for the thread you choose; select the smallest needle that you find comfortable)
- Sewing machine
- Temporary spray adhesive
- Rotary cutter
- Clear acrylic ruler, ⅛" thick, to use as a cutting guide
- Self-healing, gridded cutting mat that measures 30" x 36"

TRANSFERRING PATTERNS

There are three possible ways to transfer the design patterns for the wool appliqué projects in this book.

Method One: For simple shapes that will be used only once or twice, I recommend using tracing paper to make templates. Trace the pattern from the book onto tracing paper, cut out the template, and then pin the template to the wool. Cut out the wool piece. Do not add seam allowances to either the paper or the wool appliqué pieces.

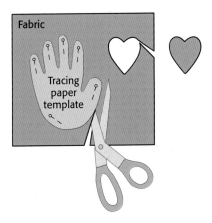

Don't try to cut the paper and the wool at the same time. Your scissors won't like it, and the edges of both the paper and the wool will be ragged. (Blanket stitches will not hide poorly cut edges.) Sharp scissors and careful craftsmanship go a long way at this stage.

Method Two: When you will be tracing the same shape many times, make your templates out of sturdy plastic template material. Use the lightweight template plastic sold in quilt shops or a plastic of similar weight. Trace the pattern from the book onto the plastic sheet and cut out the template. Do not add seam allowances. Using a chalk pencil, draw around the template on the wool. You must hold the template firmly because wool has a tendency to stretch and pull. Cut the wool on the chalk line.

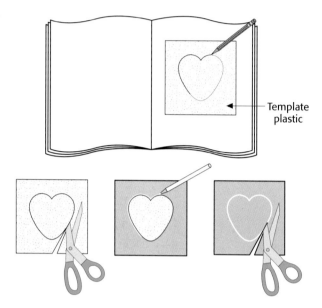

Template plastic

Method Three: For pattern pieces that are highly detailed or that will be used many times, I recommend using a lightweight, nonfusible interfacing for the template. Trace the pattern from the book directly onto the interfacing. Cut out the interfacing, pin the interfacing to the wool, or use temporary adhesive spray to hold the shape in place. Then cut out the wool piece and remove the interfacing.

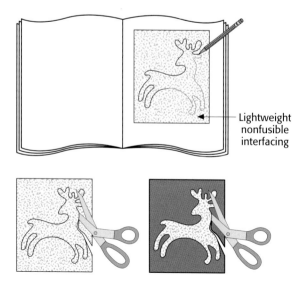

Lightweight nonfusible interfacing

STITCHING

The blanket stitch is the most commonly used stitch for all of the wool quilts. Pin, baste, or spray baste the appliqué piece in place, and then stitch. To spray baste, use temporary spray adhesive on the wrong side of the appliqué piece and position the piece on the background. Be sure to catch both the appliqué and the background layers of fabric with each stitch. I usually use two strands of embroidery floss when I work with wool appliqué. If you use perle cotton, size number 8 works best. Lower numbers are heavier and more difficult to stitch with.

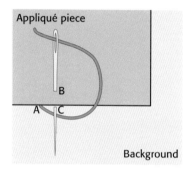

Appliqué piece

B
A C

Background

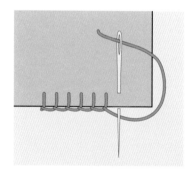

Try to keep your stitches in uniform proportions throughout the piece. If you begin by making your stitches tall and close, keep using that same proportion, even on a smaller appliqué piece.

Strive for this:

Large piece   Medium piece   Small piece

Not this:

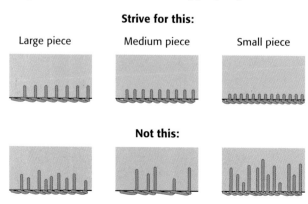

Other stitches used for details and embellishment are the chain stitch, fly stitch variation, running stitch, lazy daisy stitch, French knot, satin stitch, and star stitch.

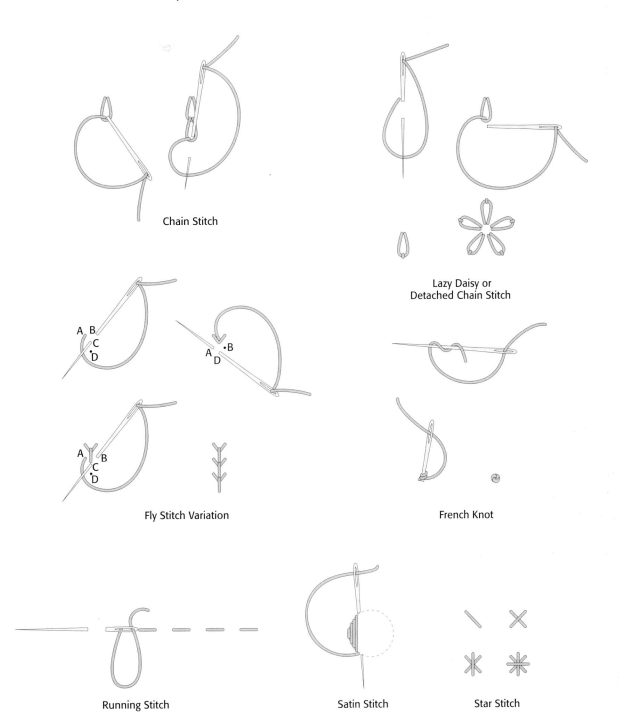

Chain Stitch

Lazy Daisy or
Detached Chain Stitch

Fly Stitch Variation

French Knot

Running Stitch

Satin Stitch

Star Stitch

My Favorite Thimble

My favorite thimble is a rubber finger guard sold at the local office-supply store! I use it for both appliqué and quilting.

Mini-Fuse Cotton Appliqué

Use this technique when working with cotton fabrics. It is basically the same thing as fusible appliqué, but because I cut away much of the fusible web before fusing, I call it "mini-fuse appliqué." This process eliminates any stiffness in your quilt from the fusible web.

Before beginning, prewash all your cotton fabric to remove any sizing. The finished appliqué piece will be the reverse of what you trace. If you want an animal positioned in a certain direction, trace it facing in the opposite direction. Remember to trace all letters backward when using the fusible technique. Refer to the fusible-web manufacturer's instructions when you are ready to fuse the appliqué pieces in place.

1. Trace the pattern onto the smooth, paper side of the lightweight fusible web. Leave a generous ½" around each traced pattern.

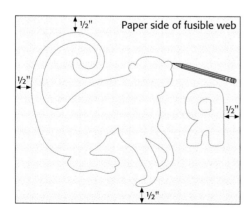

2. Cut out the fusible web from the center of the figure, ⅛" inside the traced line, all around the edges. Also leave a ⅛"-wide "border" around the inside of any areas that will be cut out. Connect these areas with "bridges" so that the inner cutout border won't separate from the outer area.

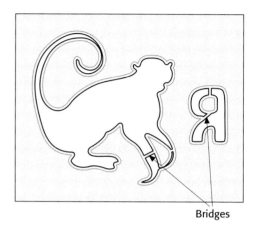

Bridges

Mini-Fuse Cotton Advice

I find that a ⅛" border works well with the blanket stitch I sew. If your blanket stitch is larger, you can cut a more generous border. I don't recommend going any smaller than ⅛".

3. Press the fusible web to the wrong side of the cotton fabric. (This is when the need for the generous ½" of fusible web around the traced figure becomes obvious. The extra fusible web holds the shape of the appliqué pattern piece so that it isn't distorted when fused in place.)

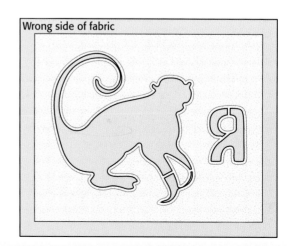

Wrong side of fabric

4. Cut out the cotton appliqué piece on the traced line. Carefully remove the paper backing and position the appliqué on the background fabric.

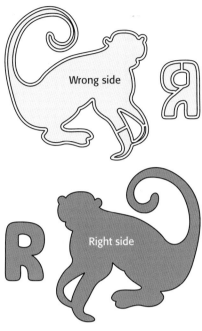

Wrong side

Right side

Ready to fuse in place

5. Don't fuse until all of the appliqué pieces are in place. This technique works for appliqué pieces of any size.

LABELING YOUR WORK

Have you ever been faced with a box of old photos with no names and no dates on the back? At the time you took the pictures, you were sure you would never forget that information. Now you can't remember, and you can be certain no one else will either! This also happens to quilts and rugs, and what a shame it is!

As timidly or as boldly as you wish, please include your name or initials and the date on your work. It makes the piece unique, special, and identifiable. For a hooked rug, I add my initials and date to the pattern with a permanent waterproof marker before I hook. That way, I won't forget to hook it in as I work.

For the wool quilts and petal and penny rugs, add the initials and date at almost any time in the creation process. For me, the best time is after all of the appliqué is done but before the project is quilted. When I do this, I can quilt around the letters and the numbers too, incorporating them into the design.

I like to sign my quilts with chain-stitched letters, but any embroidery stitch you are comfortable with will work. See "Stitching" on page 14. I embroider the letters and numbers freehand, letting them go where the needle leads me. If you prefer, draw them with chalk pencil, and then embroider them.

JCB

FINISHING THE PROJECT

Once the top is complete, you're in the home stretch. The following sections describe the steps you need to take to finish your project.

Batting and Backing

Not all the projects require batting, but when I use batting, I always choose Hobbs Thermore. It is designed especially for quilted clothing. Because it is so thin, it is easy to quilt with wool on top and a cotton backing on the bottom. I cut the batting ¼" larger than the quilt top on all four sides, but if you are new to quilting, cut it 1" or 2" all around to be safe.

Most of my backing fabrics are standard-weight, 100% cottons sold for quiltmaking. Cut the backing the same size as the batting. For all backing fabrics, be sure to prewash and dry the fabric before using.

Layering and Basting

On a flat surface, lay out the backing fabric first, with the wrong side up. Place the batting over this, making sure the edges line up. Finally, with the right side up, place the quilt top on the batting. Baste the three layers together with 1"-long dressmaking pins, a quilt basting gun, or a needle and thread. Baste closely in areas that will not be quilted.

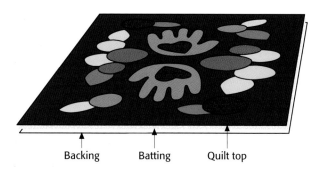

Backing   Batting   Quilt top

Quilting

The folk-style embroidery work of Eastern Europe has always had a strong influence on my designs. I think my quilting stitch reflects that. The length of the stitch or the number of stitches per inch are not what is important to me. I am most concerned with the color and the texture that the patterns create. If it takes double thread and large stitches to achieve the right effect, then that is what I do! Sometimes I want long stitches to accent a design element. Other times, I try for lots of tiny stitches to create a dimpled background. For these types of quilts, if I am happy with the effect, then I know that I chose the right stitch!

If you wish to mark the quilting lines, use chalk or another marker of your choice. Remember to test your marker on a scrap to make sure you can remove the marks. Quilt your wool quilts with two or three strands of embroidery floss or a single strand of perle cotton.

I begin my quilting in the center of the quilt and echo the shapes as I stitch around them. Because I don't work with a hoop, I tend to draw the stitches up fairly tight, an effect I like. This slightly reduces the size of the quilt, but it gives it a nice crinkled texture. The following steps explain the quilting process in detail.

1. Start with two or three strands of embroidery floss or a single strand of perle cotton, 18" long. Make a small knot at the end and insert the needle into the quilt top about ½" away from where you plan to begin quilting. Pull the needle through the batting and bring it up at the point where you want to begin the line of quilting.

2. Gently pull the knot through the top fabric, leaving it buried in the batting.

3. Using a running stitch, quilt along the line to be quilted. Your quilting stitches can be as large or as small as you like.

4. When you reach the end of your stitching, make a small knot close to the quilt and pop it through the top fabric into the batting. Bring the end of the thread out about ½" from where the thread went into the quilt and clip it.

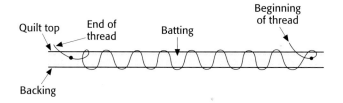

Quilt top   End of thread   Batting   Beginning of thread

Backing

Squaring Up the Quilt

After I finish the quilting but before I add the binding, I like to "square up" the quilt. This simply means that you trim the quilt so that each of the four corners is a 90° angle. This is one of the times when a gridded cutting mat is indispensable. Most of these quilts are small enough to fit on a mat with room to spare. I work on a 30" x 36" mat.

1. To square up a quilt, trim the smoothest and straightest edge of the quilt by using a rotary cutter, clear acrylic ruler, and gridded cutting mat.

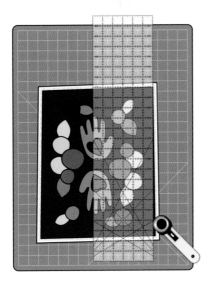

2. Place the cut edge along one of the grid lines on the cutting mat, lining up the next edge with a perpendicular line on the mat, and trim the second edge. The corner between these two cut edges is now 90°, or "square."

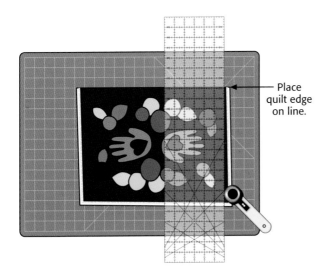

Place quilt edge on line.

3. Continue lining up the edges and trimming in this manner until all the corners are square.

Making Binding

For most of the quilts in this book, a straight-grain binding is sufficient. For quilts with rounded or irregular edges, I recommend using bias-cut binding for a smoothly finished edge. For "Petal Hearts" on page 92, I used a purchased ½"-wide, double-fold, bias-tape binding, since the background of the quilt is black and most of the edge is hidden by the petals.

For all straight-grain binding, I use 1½"-wide strips of cotton. For "Folksy Tree Skirt" on page 44, I wanted a narrower edge and used 1¼"-wide bias strips for the binding. You can use wool if you want, but it is bulky.

To make straight-grain binding, cut strips across the width of the fabric, from selvage to selvage. Stitch strips together end to end with a diagonal seam to make one continuous strip of binding. Trim the excess fabric and press the seam open.

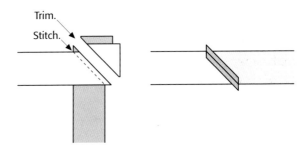

Trim.

Stitch.

To make bias binding, I frequently use a fat quarter. Press the fabric, making sure the edges are cut straight with the grain of the fabric.

1. Fold over one corner of the fabric diagonally to find the "true bias" (the line that runs at a 45° angle to the straight grain).

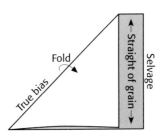

Fold

Selvage

Straight of grain

True bias

2. Cut along this fold line, and then use it as a guide to rotary cut the number of 1½"-wide strips needed to bind the quilt.

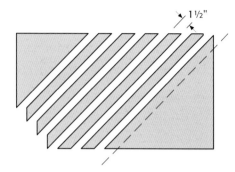

3. Stitch the pieces together as shown to make one continuous bias strip. Press the seams open.

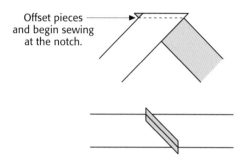

Attaching Binding

The following steps describe how to attach your binding to the project.

1. With right sides together, line up the raw edges of the binding and the quilt top. Fold the beginning of the binding back ½" over itself and pin in place as shown. Stitch with a ¼"-wide seam allowance along one side of the quilt, stopping ¼" from the edge. Backstitch and clip the threads.

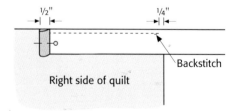

2. Remove the quilt from the machine. Fold the binding away from the quilt, perpendicular to the edge you just stitched. Then fold it back down along the next edge to be stitched.

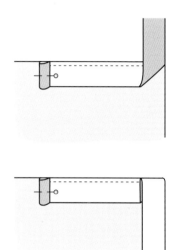

3. Starting at the top, stitch down the next side until you come within ¼" from the next edge. Backstitch.

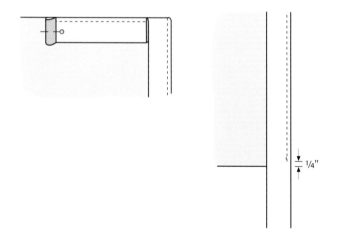

4. Repeat the corner turns. After you stitch the binding to the quilt all the way around, overlap the binding about ¼" over the fold at the beginning. Trim the extra binding, and then finish stitching the binding to the quilt.

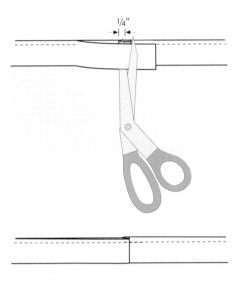

5. Turn the binding over to the back of the quilt and fold under ¼" along the raw edge. Pin and slip-stitch in place. This hem will cover the machine stitching, and the corners will form folded miters.

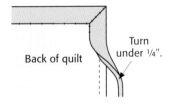

STEAM PRESSING

A final pressing with steam gives the quilt a crisp finish that I find attractive. Here's how to give your quilts that professional finish.

1. Dampen a large piece of muslin slightly. Wring it out well—it should not be dripping wet.

2. Place your quilt on an ironing board, right side down. Cover it with the damp cloth. Press, with the iron set at "wool." Gently move the iron around the muslin press cloth, being careful not to stretch or distort the quilt. A steam iron is not necessary since the damp cloth will provide all of the steam necessary. I press just until the muslin press cloth is dry.

3. Remove the press cloth and allow the quilt to cool on the ironing board or other flat surface for 5 to 10 minutes, or until completely cool and dry.

RUG-HOOKING ESSENTIALS

If you have been doing wool appliqué and want to add rug hooking to your fun bag of tricks, you probably have a stash of the first requirement—wool! If not, be sure to read the section "All about Wool" on page 6, and then come back here to learn the basics about materials, equipment, and techniques.

Estimating Wool Yardage

Amounts given in most rug-hooking patterns are approximate. Depending on the width of your strips, the height of your loops, and how closely you pack your loops, you may require different amounts of wool than those specified in the pattern.

When you try a project of your own design or a pattern where yardage amounts are not included, follow this rule of thumb: multiply the area you plan to cover with wool by 5 to find the amount of wool you need. For example, if the pattern has a small house about 3" wide and 2" high, the total area to cover is 6 square inches. So, you will need 5 times that number, or a total of 30 square inches of wool to hook the house. Wool amounts for the rugs in this book are generously estimated and allow for 5 times the area to be covered.

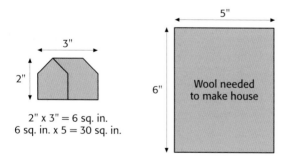

2" x 3" = 6 sq. in.
6 sq. in. x 5 = 30 sq. in.

Wool needed to make house

Although the wool yardages are based on a 54" width, keep in mind that in rug hooking, any size piece of wool is usable. If you need 500 square inches of

green, that could be 1 rectangle, measuring 20" x 25"; 20 squares, each measuring 5" x 5"; or 1 strip, measuring 2" x 250"! Each way, you have 500 square inches, and all of the wool can be put to good use.

Color placement also affects the amount of wool needed. If, for example, you choose to use a different color than the pattern recommends, you must make adjustments based on the calculations given above.

Of course, not all of the design elements of a rug come in easy-to-measure rectangular shapes, so a great deal of "guesstimation" must occur. But take heart! Some of the most successful rugs are created by running out of a specific color of wool and not being able to match it with a new supply. Necessity is certainly the mother of invention at moments like those.

One way to disguise an unplanned color change is to introduce a new color slowly, mixing the old and new colors and gradually changing to the new color.

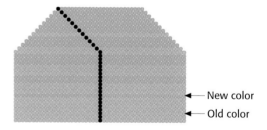

← New color
← Old color

Another trick is to alter the design, adding an inner border or another design element. In my very first rug, I ran out of the original background color after only the center portion was hooked. I introduced a ribbon-like border around that area and started a new color outside of it. Then I ran out of that color too! Next, I added a wreathlike border of flowers and started my third background. By then, I was taking no chances, so I made the final border a two-tone stripe. The results were unexpected, but it is still one of my favorite hooked pieces.

My first hooked rug

FOUNDATION FABRICS

The foundation fabric you use for your rug is just as important as the wool you hook into it. The easiest fabric to learn on and the most readily available is burlap. Burlap's stiffness makes it easier for a beginner to catch on to the rhythm of hooking and makes it harder to overpack loops (pulling too many loops through the fabric), which makes a rug wavy and lumpy. Look for even-weave Scottish burlap, which is specially woven for rug hooking. Don't be tempted to try the weak and irregular all-purpose burlap at your local craft shop. I can relate countless tales of woe about weak foundation fabrics falling apart, sometimes before the rug is completely hooked. As in quilting, the cost of the fabric you invest in a project is small compared to your time. Strive to work with the best fabric you can.

After their first rug, most rug hookers have a feel for the basic rug-hooking techniques. For the next rug, I recommend using 100%-cotton monk's cloth or linen as a foundation fabric. Monk's cloth is my favorite. It is soft to the touch, and it is easy to pull loops through the fabric. Its only disadvantage is that it is also easy to overpack. You can solve this problem easily by simply removing some of the loops in the lumpy areas. Pull carefully from the top of the rug, and then trim the strip even with the tops of the other loops.

Linen foundation fabric looks like and is as easy to use as burlap. It is twice the price of burlap but still a bargain when you consider the time you will invest. One drawback of linen is that the linen fibers sometimes migrate or "beard" to the top of the rug, just as some battings do on quilts. In a light-colored rug, this is not noticeable, but it is annoying against a dark background.

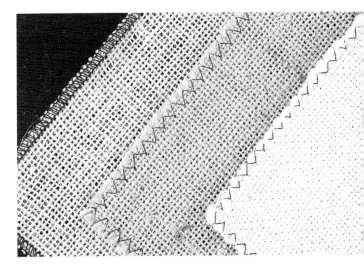

Foundation fabrics for rug hooking include (from left to right) linen, burlap, and monk's cloth.

As you can see from these pros and cons, the right foundation fabric for you is the fabric that you find easy to work with and that provides the desired results. When purchasing any foundation fabric, plan on at least 3" extra on all sides of the design. In the materials lists for the projects in this book, I have allowed 4" all around.

TOOLS

As with all crafts, rug hooking has a few basic tools that make the job easier.

Hooking Frame: You can get by with using a regular quilting hoop or by pinning the foundation to a padded picture frame. Both are excellent options for a person with three hands! For the rest of us, starting with a quilting hoop on a floor stand or lap stand works well. The stand eliminates the need for the third hand.

The best option by far is a frame designed specifically for rug hooking. The Puritan frame has been around for many years and will last and last and last. I have one that I purchased nearly 20 years ago and I also have the one my grandma purchased over 40 years ago, and the two frames look identical! This frame comes with two adjustable sides for tightening the foundation fabric on the frame. You can also purchase a floor stand to hold this frame.

Some people insist that the frame be used on a tabletop or a stand. I prefer to hold the frame in my lap, which is probably why I like the lightweight and affordable Appleton frame best of all. It does not have adjustable sides, but I have no trouble keeping the monk's cloth stretched tight.

Both the Appleton and Puritan frames are constructed with four strips of metal needle boards, also called carding strips, metal Velcro, or gripper strips. They are short and prickly and work like a dream.

Puritan frame with gripper strips

Hook: The hook most commonly used for making rugs looks like a crochet hook with a wooden handle. I work with the most comfortable hook I own, the one my Grandma gave to me nearly 20 years ago. Purchase the hook that fits your hand and hooking style the best. I suggest trying different styles to see which you prefer.

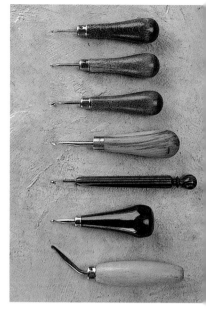

Various styles of hooks

Cutter: It is possible to use a rotary cutter to cut your wool strips but only for the wider widths of ¼" used in primitive rugs. Even then, the wool moves around under the ruler and is difficult to control. You can also cut wool strips by hand with scissors, but it is time-consuming and again only worth the effort if you want the look of a very primitive type of rug. There are three commercial cutters available today. The Bliss, Rigby, and Fraser cutters are all excellent machines and very similar in price. The Bliss model attaches to a tabletop with suction cups. The Rigby and Fraser machines are similar to each other, and each machine clamps to a tabletop. (See page 111 for information on ordering cutters and other rug-hooking equipment.)

Fraser cutter

Rigby cutter

CUTTING STRIPS

Cutters for rug hooking come with interchangeable cutting heads that cut strips of wool from ³⁄₃₂" wide (#3 cut) to ¼" (#8 cut) or wider.

Cut Number	Cut Strip Width
3	³⁄₃₂"
4	⅛"
5	⁵⁄₃₂"
6	³⁄₁₆"
8	¼"

The width of the wool strips greatly affects the look of the rug. The narrower the cut, the more loops you must make. This way, you can achieve more detail. Depending on the weave of your foundation fabric, narrow strips (such as a #3 cut) may require that you make a loop in almost every space in the foundation fabric. Wider strips require skipping more spaces. For the projects in this book, most strips are cut ⅛" or ⁵⁄₃₂" wide.

Before cutting strips, tear the wool into strips 3" or 4" wide. It is much easier to feed this size strip through the cutter than to wrestle with a wider piece. Use any length that you find comfortable.

Tearing the wool instead of cutting it serves an important purpose. The torn edge gives a straight edge that follows the lengthwise or crosswise threads in the fabric, giving it greater strength when it is cut into strips. If the wool is not cut on the straight edge

of the fabric, it will come apart with a gentle tug after being cut into a narrow strip.

Wool cut along straight edge

Wool cut at angle to straight edge

If you know which way is the lengthwise grain of the wool, it is preferable to cut along it rather than across it. If you aren't sure, either crosswise or lengthwise will probably be all right. Cut two test strips in opposite directions and pull gently on them to see if there is a difference in strength.

When cutting plaids and stripes, you can cut along the "stripes" of the pattern to get solid strips of different colors. If you cut across the pattern, you will get multicolored strips. Hook a small sample swatch of each to see the varied results you can get from one piece of wool.

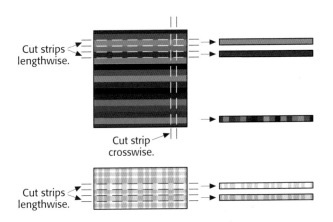

Cut strips lengthwise.

Cut strip crosswise.

Cut strips lengthwise.

Develop the habit of reversing the direction and flipping your wool as you run it through the cutter to make successive cuts. The end that went through the cutter last should be turned over (top side on the bottom) and fed through the cutter first for the next cut. That makes it easier to keep your cuts straight with the grain of the fabric.

ORGANIZING WOOL STRIPS

Keep your wool strips organized by using one or more of the following methods. In addition to keeping colors separated, these methods are helpful for keeping different shades of one color in order.

Method One: Make deep accordion folds in stiff paper. Place a different color or shade in each section. To store the strips, fold up and secure with a ribbon or a rubber band.

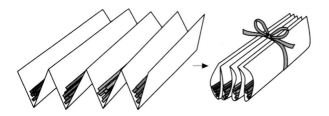

Method Two: Keep colors sorted by placing bunches of strips in pages of magazines or catalogs.

Method Three: Sew a ribbon or fabric tape to a dishtowel or fasten with safety pins. Tuck the strips in the openings. Roll and tie to store.

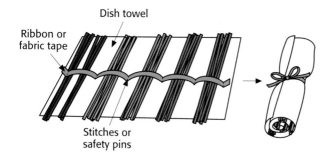

Dish towel

Ribbon or fabric tape

Stitches or safety pins

PREPARING THE FOUNDATION

The patterns in this book will need to be enlarged. Use the grid behind the pattern as a guide for enlarging the pattern by hand, or use a photocopier and enlarge by the percentage indicated. Once the pattern is enlarged, use a light table to transfer the pattern design lines onto the foundation. If you do not have a light table, you can make one by setting a piece of glass or transparent plastic between two tables (or remove a leaf from one table) and putting a lamp underneath. Be sure to use a permanent marking pen to draw the pattern.

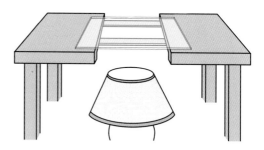

1. Place the foundation fabric over the pattern and trace the design onto the foundation fabric with a permanent marking pen.

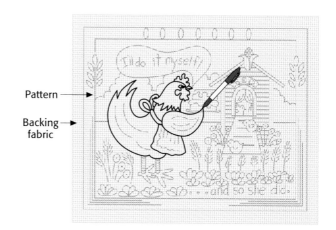

Pattern

Backing fabric

2. To prevent fraying, secure the edges of the foundation fabric with zigzag stitches, several rows of straight stitches, or masking tape.

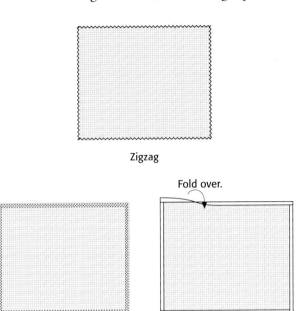

Zigzag

Straight stitches

Fold over.

Masking tape

A PERSONAL TOUCH

Don't try to copy a hooked rug pattern, loop for loop, as you would for counted cross-stitch, needlepoint, or latch-hook patterns. Rug hooking is personal and no two people hook exactly alike.

HOOKING

There is no exact order in which you must hook the different areas of the rug. I usually start in the middle and work my way to the edges, first outlining each shape, and then filling it in with rows of stitches. It is best to hook tiny details in an area first and then immediately fill in around them to help hold and define their shape.

1. With the design side up, place the foundation fabric in the quilting hoop or on the hooking frame. If you are hooking on burlap or linen, the fabric only needs to be snug in the frame or hoop. When working with monk's cloth, keep your fabric very taut to avoid overcrowding or overpacking the loops.

PROBLEM SOLVER

If the foundation is too small to fill the hoop or frame, sew scraps of any extra fabric to the edges of the foundation fabric to make it large enough.

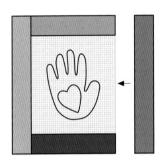

2. Hold the hook in your right hand like a pencil. (Reverse the instructions if you are left-handed.) As you work, you can try different grips to see what works best for you. Begin in a center section of the rug.

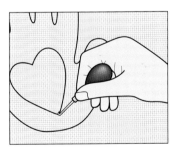

3. Hold a strip of wool fabric in your left hand between the thumb and forefinger underneath the foundation and frame or hoop. Insert the hook through the top of the pattern. With the barb of the hook, catch the wool strip underneath and pull the end of the wool out to the top of the pattern, leaving about ½" sticking out.

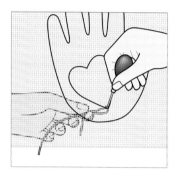

4. Insert the hook in the next hole of your fabric and draw up a loop of wool. Use the hand underneath to guide the wool as it is being pulled up by the hook and to make sure it doesn't twist and there are no loops on the back of the rug. Make each loop as high as the wool is wide. As you pull up on the new loop, always pull toward the loop you just hooked.

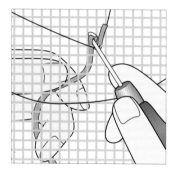

5. Continue in this manner, trying to make each loop the same height. Do not try to make a loop in every single hole. You can skip every fourth or fifth hole, but this depends on the foundation fabric, wool size, and other factors. If you pack the loops too closely, the rug will get lumpy. If they are hooked too loosely, you will see "holidays" of foundation fabric peeking through. You should not be able to see backing fabric on the top of your rug. With practice you will get a feel for the just-right spacing between the loops.

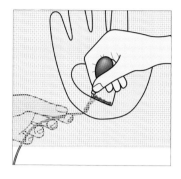

HOOKING WARM-UP

For your first rug-hooking project, I recommend that you hook a few practice rows outside the rug's border. After hooking a couple of rows—up and down, back and forth—you will be ready to start your rug.

6. When you come to the end of a wool strip, pull the tail end to the top. Pull the end of the new strip up through that same hole, once again leaving a little tail, and then continue hooking. After a few loops are hooked around the tails, trim the ends even with the tops of the loops.

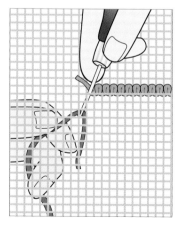

7. Outline the area to be hooked, and then fill in with one or more colors as desired. Continue outlining and hooking each area from the center outward to the edges.

Stopping and Starting

If you need to move a color across an already-hooked area, don't cross wool strips over hooked areas on the back side of your work. When you finish hooking in one area, pull the wool to the top and clip; then begin again in the new area. This keeps the back from becoming lumpy and prevents loops on the back, which are easily caught and pulled out.

Finishing the Rug

You're almost done! There is only one more process before your new heirloom is complete.

1. Stay stitch or zigzag stitch the backing fabric 1" from the edge of the hooking. Trim the excess.

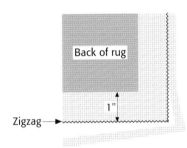

2. Fold the corner of the rug to the back. Then fold each side up to form a mitered corner.

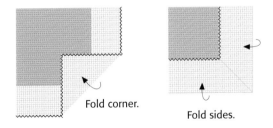

Fold corner.

Fold sides.

3. Whipstitch the fabric to the back of the rug.

Whipstitch hem to back of rug.

4. Sew rug tape over the hem if desired by using a whipstitch. Sew one edge of the tape close to the last row of hooking and the other edge to the back of the rug, covering the hem of the foundation fabric and mitering the corners.

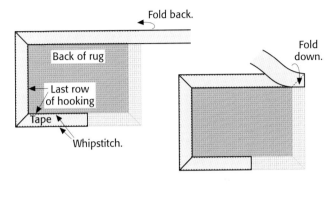

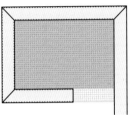

Rug Care

*   Roll rugs with the right side out. Never fold.

*   Store rugs with lavender soap or sachets to prevent insect damage and to keep the rugs fresh and sweet.

*   Gently spot clean as needed. If you must use a vacuum cleaner to clean a rug, choose a type without beaters and spinning brushes!

*   Place a nonslip rug underlay under the rug for safety. Cut it slightly smaller than the finished rug size. Most department stores carry this product. There is a rug underlay for use on smooth floors and a different underlay for carpeted floors.

APPLIQUÉ QUILTS

Before you begin any project, be sure to read "All about Wool" beginning on page 6 for selecting and prewashing wool. In the materials lists for each project, dimensions given are for prewashed wool pieces. The yardage requirements for wool are based on 54"-wide wool after prewashing and shrinking. Cotton yardage is based on 42"-wide fabric. Also keep in mind the following information:

- Unless otherwise indicated, sew all seams with ¼"-wide seam allowances.
- Sew around all of the edges of an appliquéd piece, even the parts that are partially covered by other pattern pieces. This helps the wool pieces lie nice and flat.

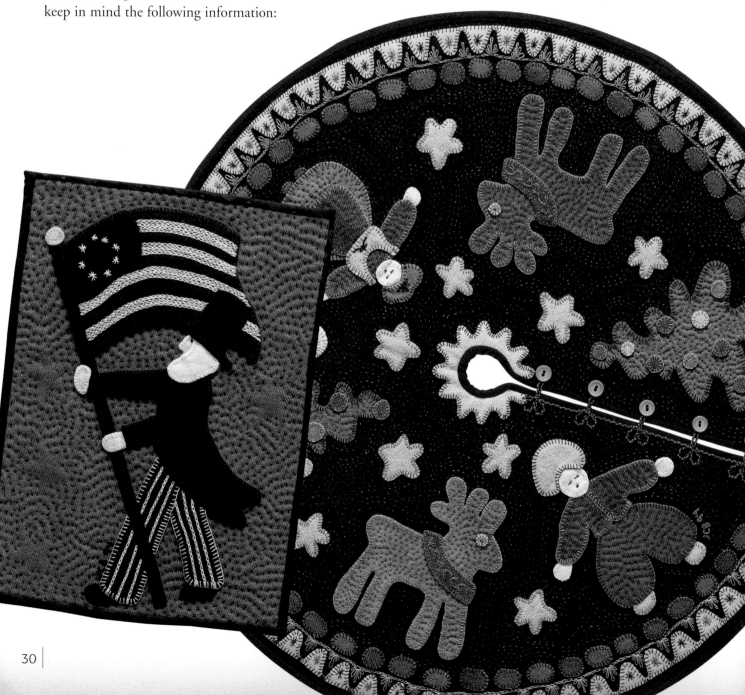

FLOWERS AND HEARTS

Finished size: 10" x 13"

This is the wool quilt that started it all for me many years ago. The heart-in-hand motif is found in many cultures throughout history. To me, it symbolizes how near and dear we must always hold life and love.

The materials needed for this quilt are a little of this and a little of that, so it's a perfect project for beginners or those who have plenty of scraps on hand.

MATERIALS

Dimensions given are for prewashed wool.
- 10" x 13" piece of wool for background
- 5" x 10" piece of wool for hands
- 4" x 6" piece of light green wool for leaves C and I
- 4" x 6" piece of dark green wool for leaves D and J
- 3" x 6" piece of wool for flower E
- 3" x 6" piece *each* of wool in 2 colors for flowers F and G
- 2" x 6" piece of wool for hearts
- 2" x 4" piece *each* of wool in 3 colors for flowers A, B, and H
- ½ yard of cotton fabric for backing and binding
- 12" x 15" piece of lightweight batting
- Embroidery floss or perle cotton in coordinating colors

CUTTING AND ASSEMBLY

1. Using the patterns on page 33, make templates and prepare the wool pieces for appliqué. See "Transferring Patterns" on page 13 for additional details.

2. Pin the wool shapes to the background fabric, referring to the quilt diagram above right for placement.

3. Working from the bottom to the top layers with three strands of embroidery floss, appliqué the hands, hearts, leaves C, D, I, and J, and flowers A, B, E, F, G, and H. Use a blanket stitch for all the pieces except flowers B, F, and H. Appliqué

these flowers by using a chain stitch around the edges. See "Stitching" on page 14 for details.

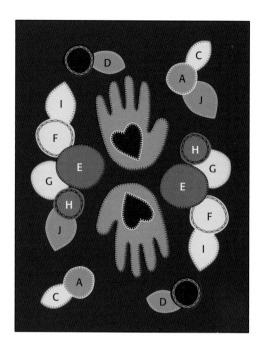

STITCHING TIP

Leave all the pieces pinned in place as much as possible when you work. Remove pins or turn back only those parts of the appliqué shapes that are in the way of your stitching.

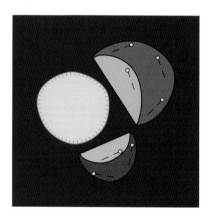

4. Embroider the centers of flowers B, F, and H with chain stitching as shown. Embroider a lazy daisy stitch in the center of the E flowers. For leaves C and I, embellish with a fly stitch variation. Add center veins to leaves D and J with the chain stitch. Refer to "Stitching" on page 14 for details.

5. Using the embroidery stitches of your choice, initial and date the front of your quilt. Refer to "Labeling Your Work" on page 17.

FINISHING

Refer to "Finishing the Project" on pages 17–21 for additional details.

1. Layer the quilt top with batting and backing. Pin or baste the three layers together.

2. Quilt as desired with embroidery floss or perle cotton.

3. Press the back of the quilt, placing a damp cloth between the quilt and the iron.

4. Square up the quilt and bind the edges.

5. Give the back of the quilt a final steam pressing.

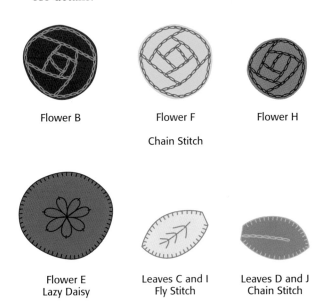

Flower B   Flower F   Flower H

Chain Stitch

Flower E
Lazy Daisy

Leaves C and I
Fly Stitch

Leaves D and J
Chain Stitch

Appliqué Patterns

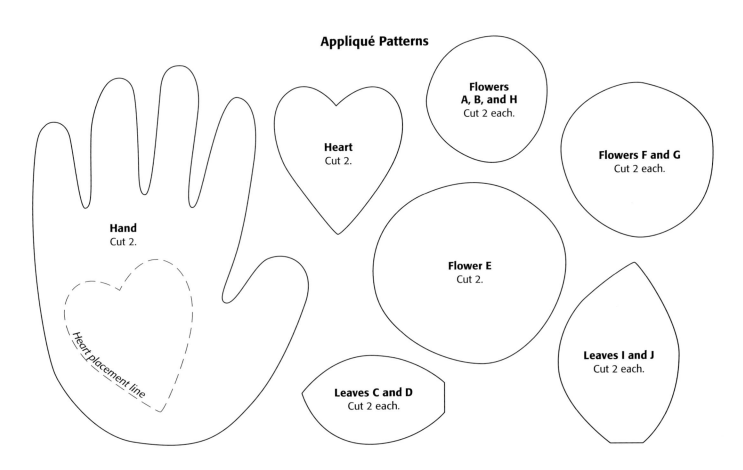

Hand
Cut 2.

Heart placement line

Heart
Cut 2.

**Flowers
A, B, and H**
Cut 2 each.

Flowers F and G
Cut 2 each.

Flower E
Cut 2.

Leaves I and J
Cut 2 each.

Leaves C and D
Cut 2 each.

UNCLE SAM

Finished size: 10" x 14"

"Uncle Sam" and "Lady Liberty" on page 39 represent a patriotic duo. Always in fashion, Uncle Sam is dressed in his snappy navy blue tails and striped red pants. I embroidered the stripes on his pants and the flag with chain stitches, but you could appliqué them if you prefer.

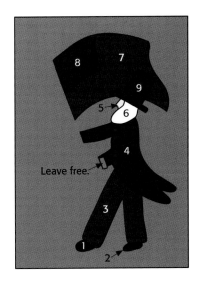

MATERIALS

Dimensions given are for prewashed wool.

- 10" x 14" piece of wool for background
- 8" x 14" piece of wool for top hat, jacket, shoes, flag corner, and flagpole
- 9" x 12" piece of wool for flag and pants
- 3" x 3" piece of wool for face and hands
- 3" x 3" piece of wool for beard
- 1" x 1" piece of wool for brass knob on flagpole
- ½ yard of cotton fabric for backing and binding
- 12" x 16" piece of lightweight batting
- Embroidery floss or perle cotton in coordinating colors

CUTTING AND ASSEMBLY

1. Using the patterns on pages 37–38, make templates and prepare the wool pieces for appliqué. See "Transferring Patterns" on pages 13–14 for additional details.

2. Pin the wool pieces to the background fabric, referring to the quilt diagram for placement.

3. Using a blanket stitch, appliqué the pieces to the quilt in the order shown above right. Begin with Uncle Sam's shoes, and then add his pants, jacket (leaving the end of the lower sleeve free for tucking the hand under later), face, and beard. Then appliqué the flag (tucking Sam's top hat out of the way), the corner of the flag, and then the top hat.

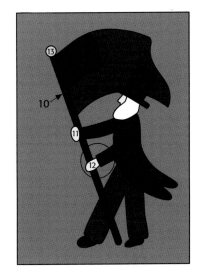

4. Appliqué the flagpole, the hands, and finally the brass knob at the end of the pole. Finish appliquéing the lower sleeve.

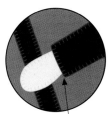

Finish lower sleeve.

5. With a chalk pencil or similar marker, draw the lines for the flag stripes and for the stripes on Uncle Sam's pants. For the flag stripes, embroider four rows of chain stitches for each stripe. For the pants, embroider one row of chain stitches for each stripe. See "Stitching" on page 14.

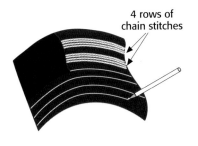

4 rows of chain stitches

Single rows of chain stitches

6. To mark the stars on the flag, use 1"-long straight pins. Arrange the pins in the center of the flag corner, as shown, and embroider a star stitch at both ends of each pin.

7. Embroider a French knot for Uncle Sam's eye.

8. Using the embroidery stitches of your choice, initial and date the front of your quilt. See "Labeling Your Work" on page 17.

FINISHING

Refer to "Finishing the Project" on pages 17–21 for additional details.

1. Layer the quilt top with batting and backing. Pin or baste the three layers together.

2. Quilt as desired with embroidery floss or perle cotton. Cut star shapes out of scrap fabric by using the pattern on page 38 and scatter them around in the background of the quilt. Pin the stars in place but do *not* appliqué them to the background. Use the fabric stars as guides only. Quilt around the stars, Uncle Sam, and the flag. Remove the fabric stars after quilting.

Remove fabric stars after quilting.

SHORTCUT

Use temporary spray adhesive to hold the stars in place while quilting. You won't have to worry about your thread catching on pin points.

3. Press the back of the quilt, placing a damp cloth between the quilt and the iron.

4. Square up the quilt and bind the edges.

5. Give the back of the quilt a final steam pressing.

"Uncle Sam" by Debra Haggard, 1994, 10" x 14". Debra appliquéd the stripes of the flag and added stars to the background.

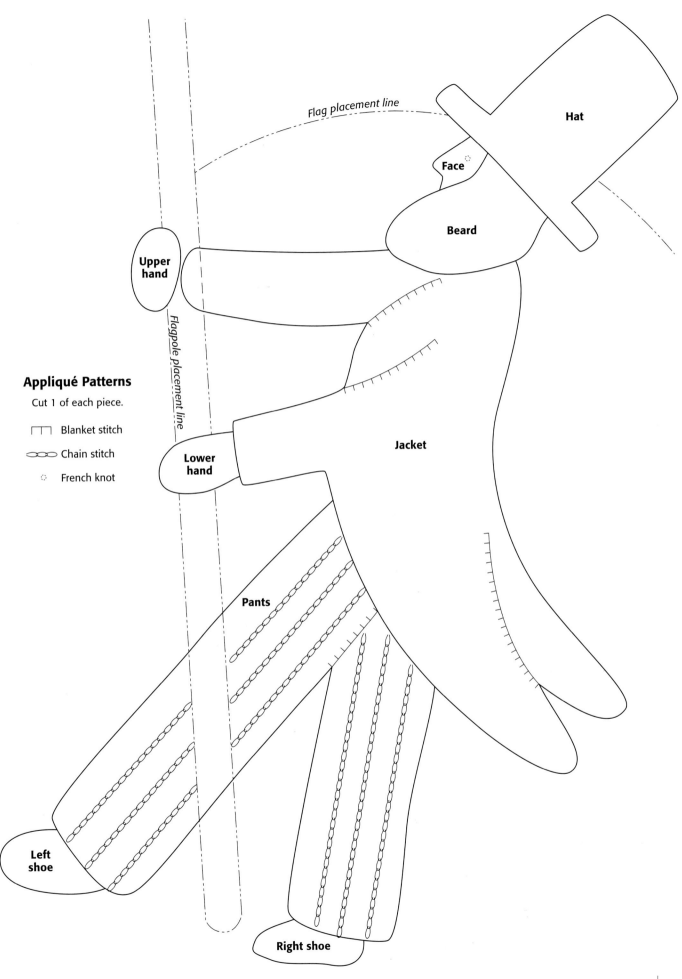

Flag placement line

Hat

Face ○

Beard

Upper
hand

Flagpole placement line

Appliqué Patterns

Cut 1 of each piece.

⊓⊓ Blanket stitch

∞∞ Chain stitch

○ French knot

Jacket

Lower
hand

Pants

Left
shoe

Right shoe

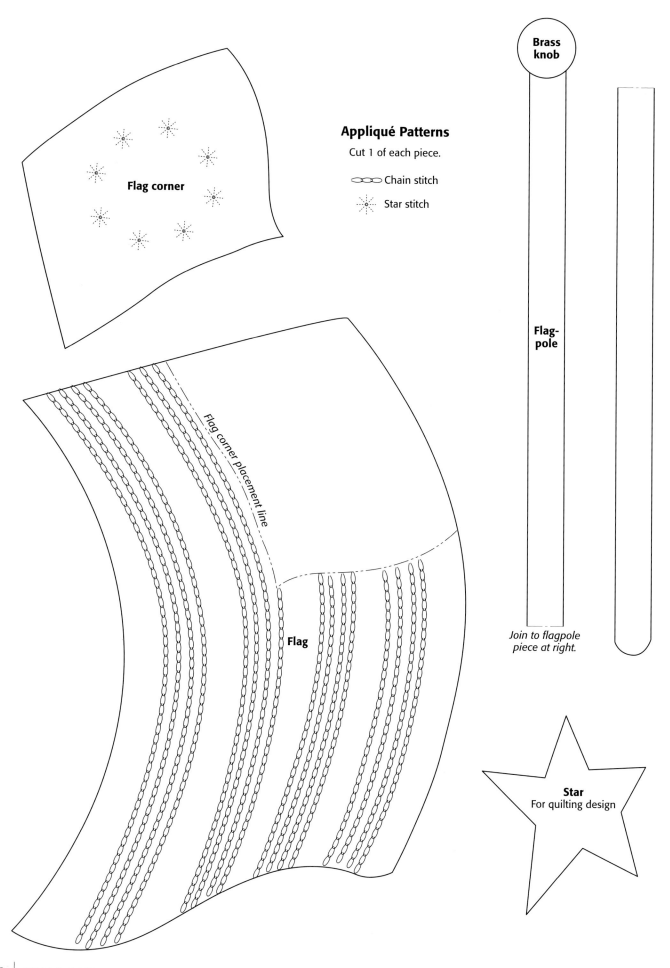

Flag corner

Appliqué Patterns

Cut 1 of each piece.

⬭⬭⬭ Chain stitch

✳ Star stitch

Flag corner placement line

Flag

Brass knob

Flag-pole

Join to flagpole
piece at right.

Star
For quilting design

LADY LIBERTY

Finished size: 10" x 14"

As I worked on this quilt and "Uncle Sam" on page 34, I nicknamed them Libby and Sam. I have used Lady Liberty in several different designs over the years, but here she is Uncle Sam's counterpart. The two designs create a balanced pair and work well together. You can combine them into one quilt on a larger background if you like.

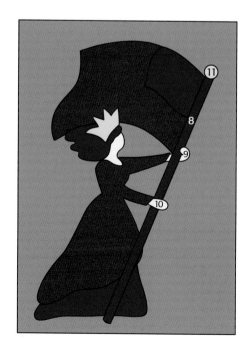

MATERIALS

Dimensions given are for prewashed wool.

- 10" x 14" piece of wool for background
- 8" x 14" piece of black wool for flag corner, hair, flagpole, and lower skirt
- 9" x 12" piece of red wool for dress and flag
- 4" x 4" piece of wool for face and hands
- 3" x 3" piece of gold wool for crown and brass knob on flagpole
- ½ yard of cotton fabric for backing and binding
- 12" x 16" piece of lightweight batting
- Embroidery floss or perle cotton in coordinating colors

CUTTING AND ASSEMBLY

1. Using the patterns on pages 42–43, make templates and prepare the wool pieces for appliqué. See "Transferring Patterns" on page 13 for additional details.

2. Pin the wool pieces to the background fabric, referring to the quilt diagram for placement.

3. Using a blanket stitch, appliqué the pieces to the quilt in the order shown. Begin with the lower skirt, face, flag, flag corner, hair, crown, and dress, leaving the sleeves free to insert the hands under them.

4. Appliqué the flagpole and hands, making sure that the hands fit naturally around the flagpole. Note that the left hand (piece 9) must go under and on top of the flagpole (piece 8). Appliqué the sleeve ends and the brass knob at the end of the flagpole.

5. With a chalk pencil or similar marker, draw the lines for the flag's stripes. Draw the crown and dress details, the stripes on Lady Liberty's dress, and the stripes on the lower skirt; refer to the pattern on page 42 for placement. Embroider four rows of chain stitches for each flag stripe, referring to step 5 on page 35 for the quilt "Uncle Sam." For the other details, embroider one row of chain stitches.

6. Refer to step 6 on page 36 for the quilt "Uncle Sam" to embroider the stars on the flag.

7. Embroider a French knot for Lady Liberty's eye.

8. Using the embroidery stitches of your choice, initial and date the front of your quilt. See "Labeling Your Work" on page 17.

FINISHING

Refer to "Finishing the Project" on pages 17–21 for additional details.

1. Layer the quilt top with batting and backing. Pin or baste the three layers together.

2. Quilt as desired with embroidery floss or perle cotton. See step 2 on page 36 of the quilt "Uncle Sam" if you want to use the same technique to quilt star shapes in the background.

3. Press the back of the quilt, placing a damp cloth between the quilt and the iron.

4. Square up the quilt and bind the edges.

5. Give the back of the quilt a final steam pressing.

"Lady Liberty" by Debra Haggard, 1994, 10" x 14". Debra added stars to the background and gave Lady Liberty a star-spangled skirt.

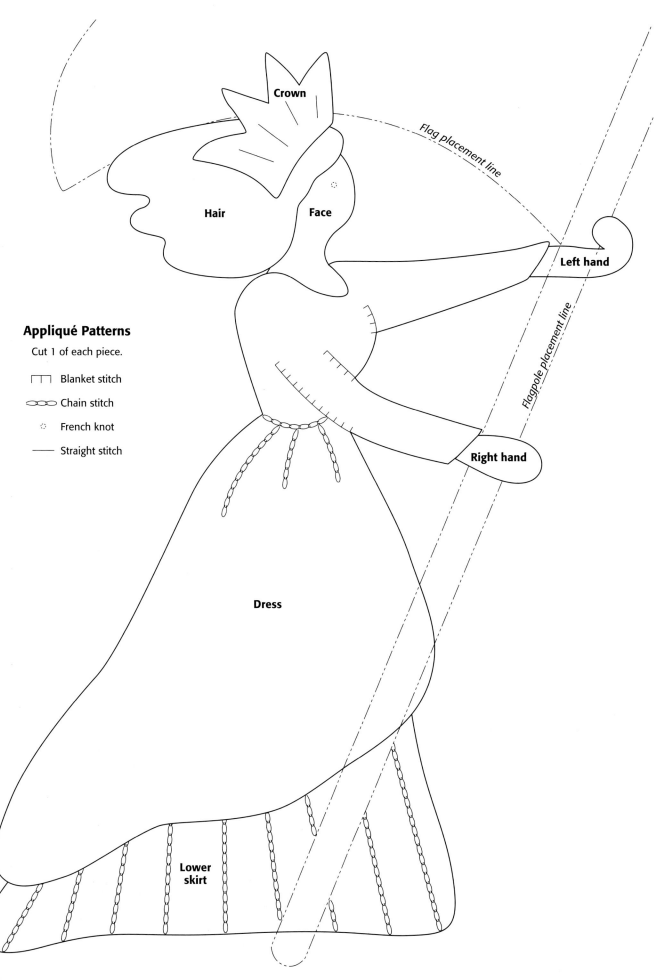

Crown

Flag placement line

Hair

Face

Left hand

Flagpole placement line

Appliqué Patterns

Cut 1 of each piece.

⊓⊓ Blanket stitch

⊂⊃⊂⊃ Chain stitch

· French knot

— Straight stitch

Right hand

Dress

Lower skirt

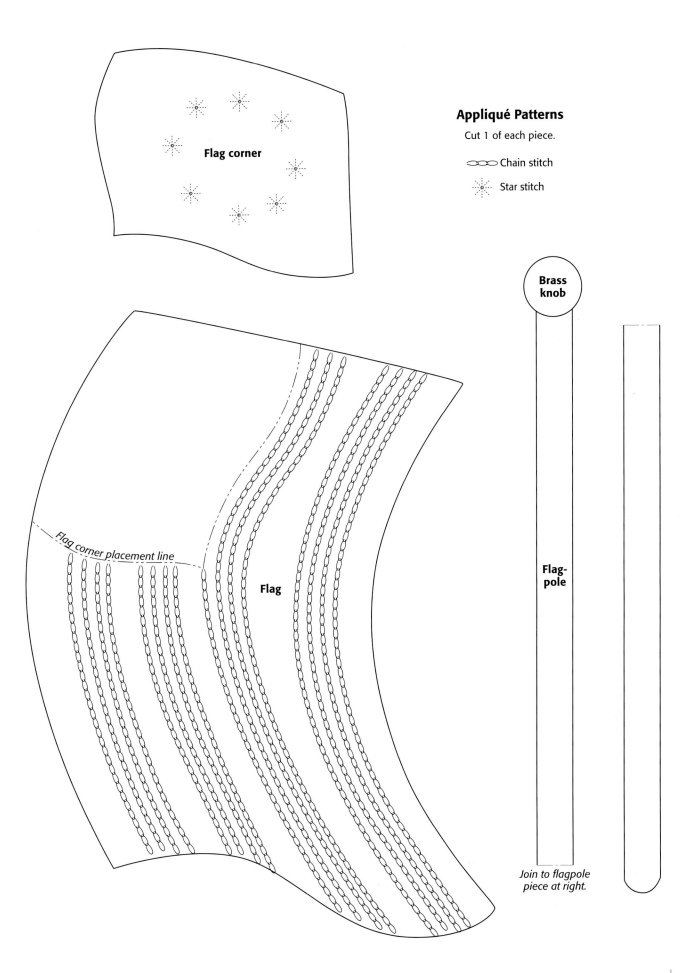

Appliqué Patterns

Cut 1 of each piece.

Chain stitch

Star stitch

Flag corner

Flag corner placement line

Flag

Brass
knob

Flag-
pole

*Join to flagpole
piece at right.*

FOLKSY TREE SKIRT

Finished size: 27" diameter

The images of Old World folk art, whether in embroidery, costumes, art, or architecture, have always fascinated and influenced me. Make this project as a tree skirt to use for the holidays, or create a circular wall quilt or table topper to enjoy all year. Embellish the sweet and rather whimsical folk images with embroidery stitching, buttons, or beads.

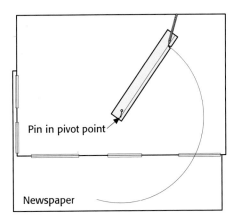

MATERIALS

Dimensions given are for prewashed wool.

- 28" x 28" piece of wool for background
- 12" x 18" piece of wool for scallops, center flower, and stars
- 10" x 14" piece of wool for trees and dots
- 10" x 10" piece *each* of wool in 4 or more assorted colors for figures, clothing, and dots
- 7" x 9" piece *each* of wool in 2 colors for reindeer
- 1 yard of cotton fabric for backing
- ½ yard of cotton fabric for binding
- 30" x 30" piece of lightweight batting
- Embroidery floss or perle cotton in coordinating colors
- 3 yards *each* of perle cotton in 3 coordinating colors for button loops*
- 5 buttons, *each* ⅝" diameter*

These are needed for the tree skirt. If you are making a circular quilt, you won't need these.

PREPARING THE CIRCLE PATTERN

You will need a paper circle pattern, 27" in diameter, for the tree skirt. Follow the steps below for my "Super-Easy Circle Maker."

1. Cut a strip of cardboard 2" x 16". Draw a line ½" from one of the long edges of the cardboard strip as shown. For any size circle, the width of the cardboard should be 2", and the length should be the radius plus 2½". (The radius is the length from the center of the circle to the outer edge.) For example, a 27"-diameter circle has a radius of 13½", so the dimensions of your cardboard strip should be 2" x 16".

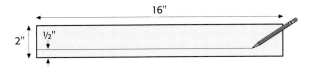

2. Now make a mark on the line ½" from the end of the cardboard strip to indicate the pivot point. Make another mark on the line 13½" from the pivot point; then cut a notch with the tip placed on the line. The point of a pencil or pen, inserted in the notch tip, will touch the line.

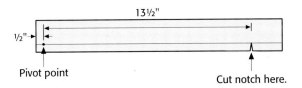

NOTE: *The pivot point and the notch tip must be the same distance from the long edge of the cardboard strip. In this case, that distance is ½".*

3. Spread out and tape together two newspaper pages and mark the approximate center. Push a pin through the pivot point of the cardboard and the center of the newspaper. With a pencil point placed in the notch tip, push the cardboard strip around to draw the circle. Cut out the circle pattern along the drawn line.

Math Tip

To determine the radius of any circle size, divide the diameter of the circle in half.

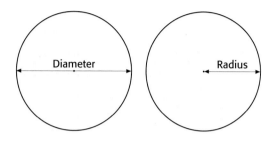

Cutting

1. **Circle:** Pin the newspaper pattern to the 28" wool square and cut out the circle. Transfer the center point from the pattern to the wool.

2. Draw a line from the center to the outer edge. This is the line you will cut along later to make the opening for the tree skirt. Try to place the line on the straight of grain, running the same direction as one set of threads in the woven fabric.

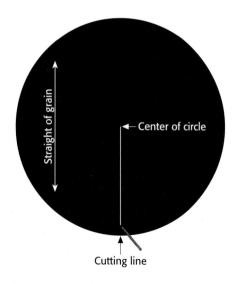

3. Baste on the cutting line. Then baste two more lines ¼" to each side of the cutting line to mark where the binding will be sewn. These lines will keep you from placing appliqué pieces too close to the binding, where they might be too bulky or visually busy.

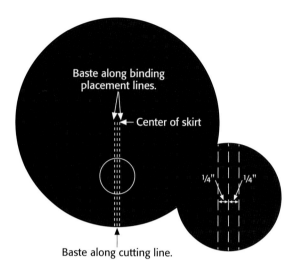

4. **Border dots:** Cut ¾"-wide strips of wool. Cut across the strips to make 1"-long pieces. Now round off the corners of each ¾" x 1" rectangle to make free-form dots. To keep the folksy nature of the design, do not make the dots identical in shape and size. You will need approximately 60 dots.

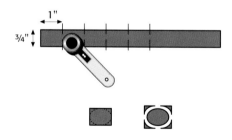

NOTE: *Later, when you arrange the dots on the background, you may find it necessary to trim some of the dots smaller in order to complete a color repeat or to fill the space nicely.*

5. **Scalloped border:** Cut 1"-wide strips of wool for the scallops. You will need a row of scallops approximately 85" long, depending on how close to the edge of the tree skirt you place them.

NOTE: *Cut the scallops from straight strips of wool fabric. It is a more efficient use of fabric, and the wool will conform to the curve. The strips can be any length you are comfortable working with or the length of the piece of fabric you are using.*

6. From the strips, cut the scallops freehand or use the pattern on page 50. Cut one end of the strip to include a narrow "connector," and cut the other end without it. The narrow connector slips under the end of the next strip, where there is no connector.

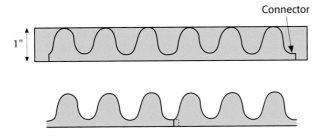

Connector

1"

7. Position the scallops and border dots around the edge of the background circle but do not appliqué them yet. When you are ready to close the circle, custom cut a few of the scallops if necessary, making them wider or narrower to fit your space. Add connectors to the ends that extend into the binding area.

Binding placement lines

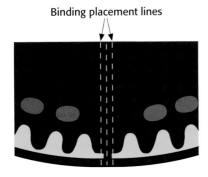

8. Using the patterns on pages 49–51, make templates and prepare the wool pieces for appliqué. See "Transferring Patterns" on page 13 for further details.

ASSEMBLY

1. Appliqué the scalloped edge and border dots, starting with the ends on each side of the basted cutting line. Do not extend the dots into the basted area.

Cutting line

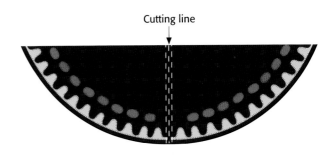

2. Place the center flower on the background, matching the center point with the center of the background.

3. Pin the remaining wool appliqué pieces to the background fabric, referring to the photograph on page 44 for placement. When you are pleased with the layout, baste the pieces in place. For smaller quilts, I usually just pin the design elements in place, but when there are this many pieces, basting is well worth the time and effort.

4. Appliqué the pieces by using the blanket stitch; refer to "Stitching" on page 14.

5. Embroider details as suggested on the pattern pages or create your own. Fill the area between the scalloped and dot borders with a chain stitch and lazy daisy variation as shown.

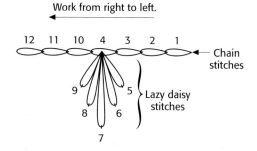

Work from right to left.

12 11 10 4 3 2 1 — Chain stitches

9   5 } Lazy daisy
8   6   stitches
   7

6. Using the embroidery stitches of your choice, initial and date the front of your quilt. See "Labeling Your Work" on page 17.

FINISHING

Refer to "Finishing the Project" on pages 17–21 for additional details.

1. Layer the quilt top with batting and backing. Pin or baste the three layers together.

2. Quilt as desired in multicolored perle cotton or embroidery floss around the central figures and even on the figures themselves if you like. Make sure none of your quilting stitches run through the basted area, or you'll cut the quilting when you cut the tree skirt opening.

3. Press the back of the quilt, placing a damp cloth between the quilt and the iron.

4. Cut the opening along the cutting line.

5. Bind the edges by using 1½"-wide, bias-cut binding strips. If you want a narrower binding, cut your binding strips 1¼" wide as I did.

6. Make a button-loop cord by braiding together three colors of perle cotton. Position the first button loop at the lower edge. Arrange and baste four more loops, each 2" apart, along the left edge of the opening. Sew the braid in place, tucking the ends of the cord under the center flower and the border dot as shown. Sew the buttons to the quilt.

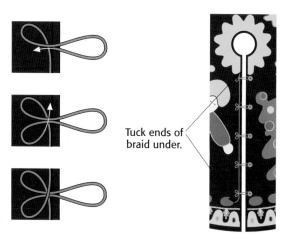

Tuck ends of braid under.

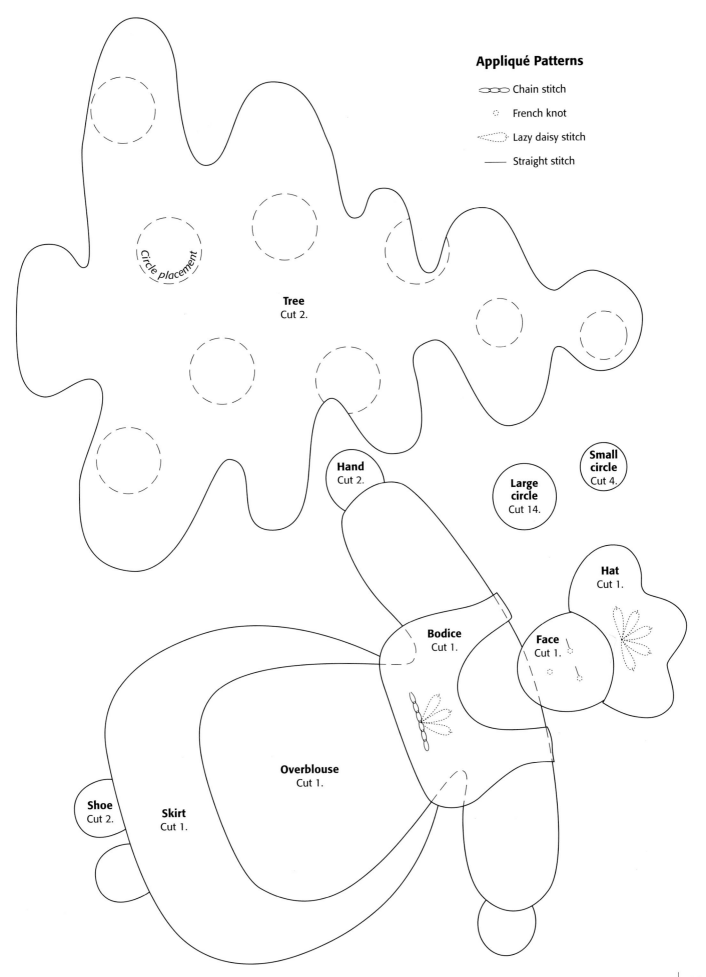

Appliqué Patterns

⬮⬮⬮ Chain stitch

∘ French knot

⬮⬮⬮ Lazy daisy stitch

— Straight stitch

Circle placement

Tree
Cut 2.

Hand
Cut 2.

Large
circle
Cut 14.

Small
circle
Cut 4.

Hat
Cut 1.

Bodice
Cut 1.

Face
Cut 1.

Overblouse
Cut 1.

Shoe
Cut 2.

Skirt
Cut 1.

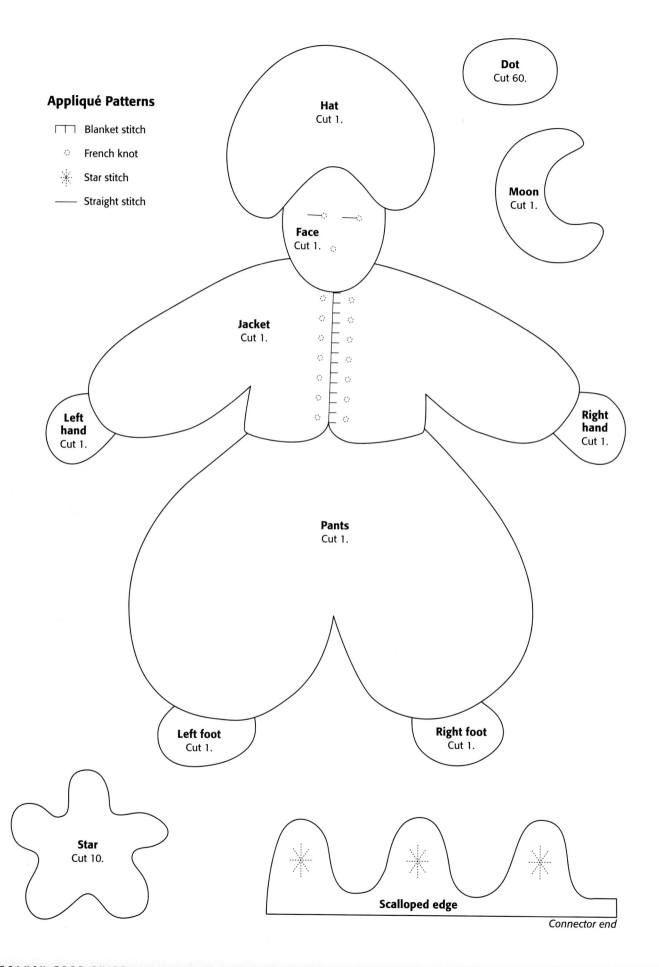

Appliqué Patterns

⊓⊓ Blanket stitch

○ French knot

✳ Star stitch

— Straight stitch

Hat
Cut 1.

Dot
Cut 60.

Moon
Cut 1.

Face
Cut 1.

Jacket
Cut 1.

Left hand
Cut 1.

Right hand
Cut 1.

Pants
Cut 1.

Left foot
Cut 1.

Right foot
Cut 1.

Star
Cut 10.

Scalloped edge

Connector end

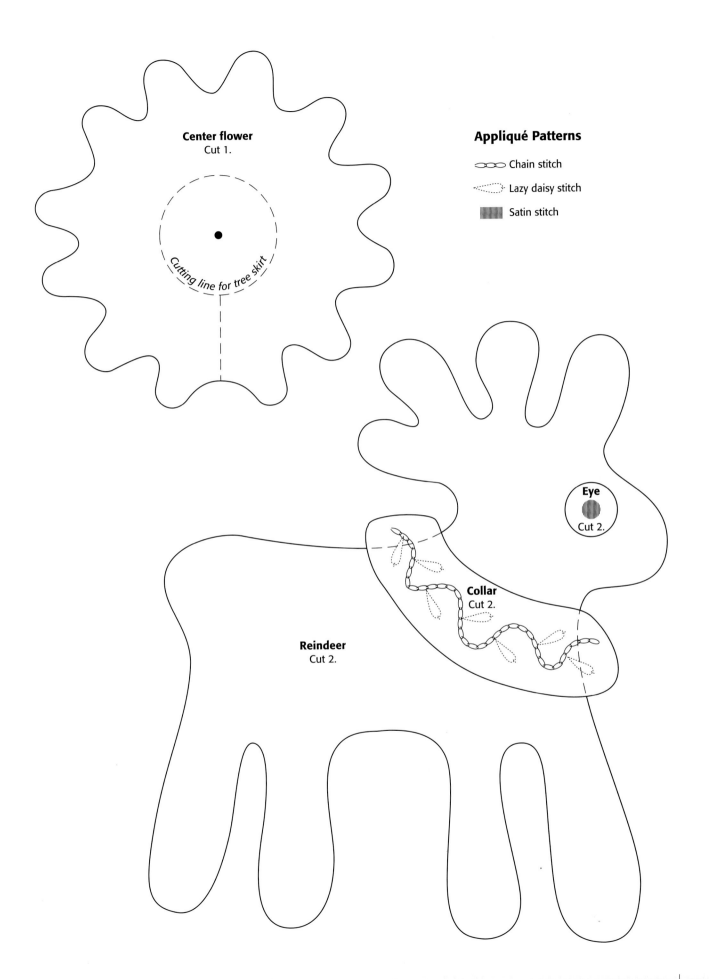

Center flower
Cut 1.

Cutting line for tree skirt

Appliqué Patterns

Chain stitch

Lazy daisy stitch

Satin stitch

Eye
Cut 2.

Collar
Cut 2.

Reindeer
Cut 2.

PENNY RUGS AND PETAL RUGS

LIKE SO many facets of our textile heritage, penny rugs have their own colorful history. At first, the word *rug* had nothing to do with a floor covering. Instead, *rugg*, as it was spelled in the early nineteenth century, meant a coarse covering for the bed or table.

During this time period, textiles were too precious for the heavy wear and tear they would receive on the floor. Hooked bed coverings and appliquéd table mats were our ancestors' early rugs, prized for their warmth and beauty. As a variety of fabrics became more widely available, hooked rugs and then penny rugs found their way to their present-day dual tasks of decoration and utility for the floor.

True penny rugs evolved shortly after the Civil War. Tradition tells us that the name comes from the coins used as a pattern to cut the many circles needed for the design. Frequently, geometric patterns of early penny rugs consisted of layers of circles, two, three, or four circles high, with each layer a little smaller than the layer under it. The blanket stitch was used to secure the circles to each other and to the background.

The choice of background fabric seemed to be a matter of either personal preference or simply whatever was on hand. Linen, wool, and cotton were all used. For my penny rug projects, I use wool on the front and line the back with cotton.

Petal, tongue, or scalloped rugs come from the same family of early American rugs that includes penny rugs. Petal rugs and penny rugs are both examples of Yankee ingenuity and making do with materials that are on hand. Traditional petal rugs do not have a batting layer and are not quilted, but they usually do have a cotton or linen backing.

CUTTING CIRCLES

THERE ARE two methods for cutting out the circles for your penny rug. The following sections describe those methods.

Method One: Tracing a Template

Use this method if you like to cut on precise lines.

1. Trace the circle pattern for your project onto lightweight template plastic. Cut out the template. Template plastic is recommended because it will hold up to repeated use better than a paper template.

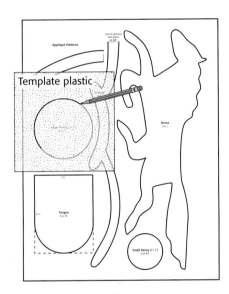

2. With a chalk pencil, trace around the circle template onto the wool. The wool fabric will stretch and pull easily, so hold the template securely on the wool as you trace.

3. Cut out each wool penny with sharp scissors.

Method Two: Freehand Cutting from Squares

Use this method if you are comfortable cutting circles freehand from squares.

1. With a rotary cutter and ruler, cut strips the same width as the diameter of the circle pattern. Crosscut the strips at the same intervals to make squares. For example, if the circle has a diameter of 2½", cut 2½"-wide strips. Crosscut the strips into 2½" squares.

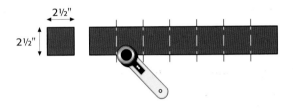

2. Cut the circles by using scissors to round off the corners of each square.

Check for accuracy and symmetry by comparing each newly cut circle with your template or the circle pattern in this book. Try to keep the cut edges very smooth. Blanket stitches won't hide ragged edges.

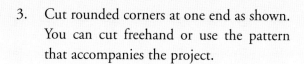

ONE WIDELY recognized characteristic of a penny rug is the tongue border. Tongues were introduced during the Victorian era when penny rugs became more richly embroidered than ever before. See "Running Horse" on page 55 for an example of a tongue border. The rounded edges of wool tongues were finished with the blanket stitch and their straight edges secured to the background fabric.

As with pennies, you can cut tongues two different ways. You can make templates from the patterns provided and trace around those, or you can cut squares or rectangles first and then round off the corners.

I often make tongues out of cotton fabric too. If you're converting a wool or felt pattern to cotton, keep in mind that cotton tongue borders require more than twice as much fabric as those made from wool or felt. You will sew two layers together and turn them right side out, which means you need two pieces for each tongue, and each piece requires a ¼"-wide seam allowance. Refer to the directions that follow to make tongues from cotton fabric.

1. Rotary cut squares or rectangles from cotton fabric as specified in the project instructions. Add ¼" extra around the curved edges of any wool tongue pattern to determine the size to cut the squares or rectangles.

2. Layer two pieces for the front and back of the tongue, keeping right sides together and aligning the edges.

Place 2 cotton rectangles
right sides together.

3. Cut rounded corners at one end as shown. You can cut freehand or use the pattern that accompanies the project.

Cut freehand or
pin the pattern in place.

4. Sew around the long curved edge with a ¼" seam allowance. Repeat, sewing next to the first line of stitching to create a double line of stitching. Trim close to the seam line.

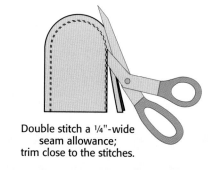

Double stitch a ¼"-wide
seam allowance;
trim close to the stitches.

5. Turn the tongue right side out and press.

RUNNING HORSE

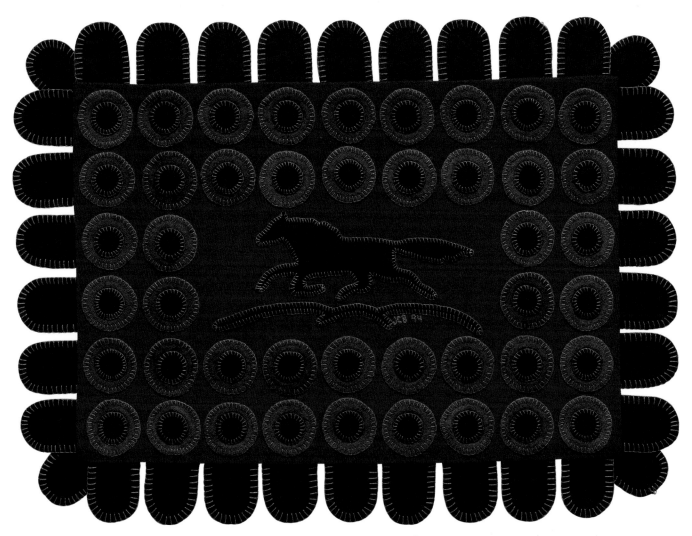

Finished size: 30½" x 22½"

Penny rugs are sometimes completely covered with circles or pennies. Other times, such as in this bold and dramatic design, pennies surround a central motif. The designs were usually inspired by daily life and could be farm animals, pets, birds, flowers, or the house itself.

MATERIALS

Dimensions given are for prewashed wool.

- 18" x 26" piece of red wool for background
- 18" x 24" piece of green wool for large pennies
- 18" x 22" rectangle of navy blue wool for tongues
- 12" x 16" piece of navy blue wool for small pennies
- 8" x 16" rectangle of navy blue wool for horse and ground
- ⅝ yard of cotton fabric for backing
- 4 skeins of gold embroidery floss

CUTTING

1. Using the tongue pattern on page 58, make a template and cut 34 tongues from the 18" x 22" piece of navy blue wool. See "Transferring Patterns" on page 13 for details.

2. From the green wool, cut 44 large pennies, and from the 12" x 16" piece of navy blue wool, cut 44 small pennies. Use one of the methods described on page 53.

ASSEMBLY

1. Stack a small navy blue penny on top of each large green penny. With the blanket stitch, appliqué the small penny to the large one, making sure that the small penny is centered on the larger one.

Make 44.

STACKING PENNIES

Baste the smaller penny onto the bottom penny with a large cross-stitch to hold it in place while stitching.

2. Arrange the penny stacks on the red wool background, referring to the photo on page 55. Cut out the horse and ground line and arrange them on the rug. (You don't want to appliqué all of the pennies in place only to find you didn't leave enough room for the horse!) Appliqué the pennies, the horse, and the ground line by using the blanket stitch.

3. Turn under the background fabric ½" toward the back of the rug, mitering at the corners. Press, always pressing on the back side and placing a damp cloth between the wool and the iron.

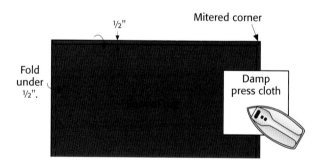

4. Blanket stitch around the long rounded edge of the tongue pieces.

5. On the back of the rug, arrange and pin or baste the tongues around the folded edge of the rug. Do not add the four corner tongues yet. Align the unstitched edge of each tongue so that it is even with the edge of the hem. Space the tongues evenly, beginning and ending ½" away from each corner.

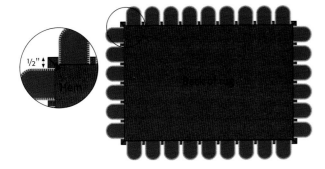

6. Turn the rug over to the front and slip-stitch the tongues in place where they join the rug.

7. Position each of the four remaining tongues diagonally at each corner. Stitch in place along the back, being careful not to stitch through to the front.

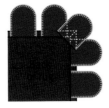

8. Using the embroidery stitches of your choice, initial and date the front of your rug. Refer to "Labeling Your Work" on page 17. Turn the rug over and press from the back.

9. With the rug placed flat, wrong side up, lay the cotton backing, right side up, over the back of the rug. Pin baste, making sure to smooth out the backing carefully from the center of the rug to the outside.

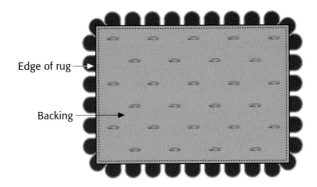

10. Fold under the edge of the backing to meet the folded edge of the front of the rug. Slip-stitch in place, and then give it a final pressing.

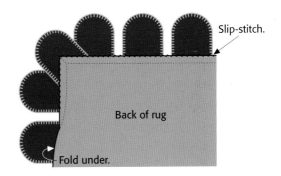

Appliqué Patterns

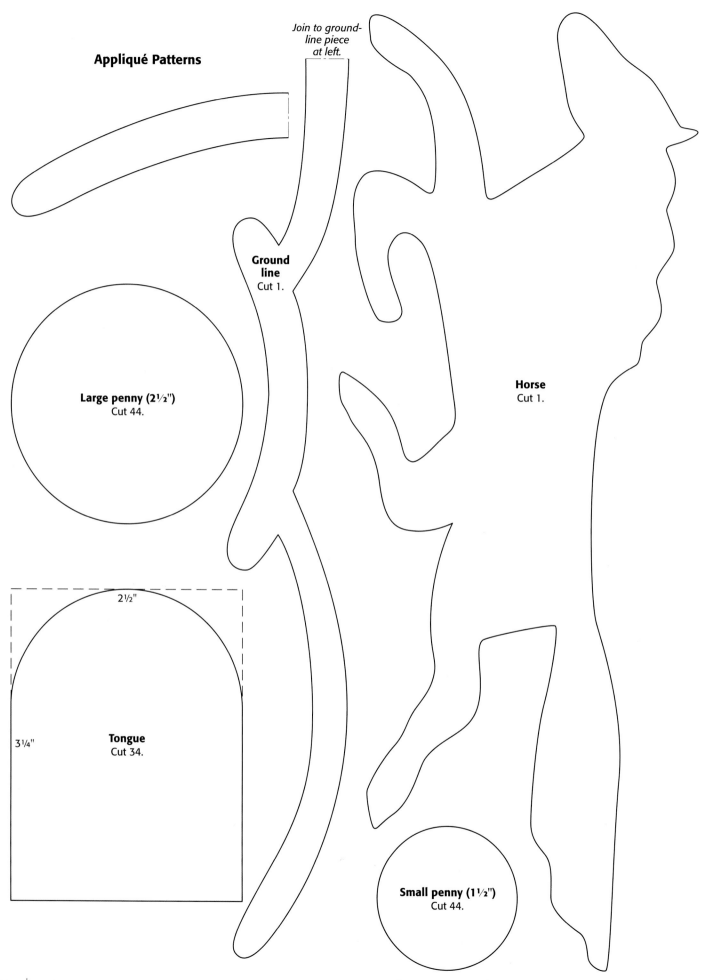

Join to ground-line piece at left.

Ground line
Cut 1.

Horse
Cut 1.

Large penny (2½")
Cut 44.

2½"

3¼"

Tongue
Cut 34.

Small penny (1½")
Cut 44.

THE LORD GOD MADE THEM ALL

Finished size: 29½" x 41½"

"All things bright and beautiful, all creatures great and small, all things wise and wonderful, the Lord God made them all." This quote from Cecil Frances Alexander was the inspiration for this bright version of a penny rug. The quilt, as well as its colorful tongue border, is all cotton. The details on the animals were added with fabric markers, but you can embroider them if you choose. This quilt can be made from any fabric; use it as a wall hanging, lap robe, or baby blanket.

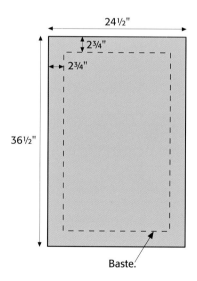

MATERIALS

Yardages are based on 42"-wide cotton fabric.

- 1 yard of yellow solid fabric for background, tongues, and binding
- ½ yard of red fabric for border
- 1 fat quarter *each* of royal blue, slate blue, gold, orange, red, green, blue-green, and purple fabric for animals, pennies, letters, and tongues
- 1 ⅛ yards of fabric for backing
- 32" x 44" piece of lightweight batting
- Lightweight fusible web
- Fabric markers
- Embroidery floss in coordinating colors

CUTTING

Before cutting any of the cotton appliqué pieces, read "Mini-Fuse Cotton Appliqué" on page 16. You will need to trace the patterns onto fusible web and fuse the web to the wrong side of the fabric before cutting. Remember to trace the letters backward when you are using the fusible appliqué technique. Refer to the patterns on pages 62–73.

From the yellow solid, cut:

- 1 piece, 24½" x 36½"
- 14 squares*, 2¼" x 2¼"
- 4 strips, 1½" x 42"

From the 8 assorted fat quarters, cut:

- 1 of each animal desired (approximately 25 total; refer to the photo on page 59)
- 20 large pennies, 1½" diameter
- 50 small pennies, ¾" diameter
- Letters for phrases around rug
- 114 squares*, 2¼" x 2¼"

From the red fabric, cut:

- 2 strips, 3" x 29½"
- 2 strips, 3" x 36½"

From the backing fabric, cut:

- 1 piece, 33" x 45"

Round 2 corners off for the tongues or make a template with the pattern on page 62. If using wool, cut half as many pieces, each 1¾" x 2".

ASSEMBLY

1. Prepare the background by basting a guideline 2¾" inside each edge of the 24½" x 36½" piece of yellow fabric. This will mark the border area for the letters.

![Diagram of yellow fabric piece 24½" x 36½" with 2¾" basting guidelines inside each edge, labeled "Baste."]

2. Remove the paper backing from the animals and arrange them on the background fabric inside the basted lines.

3. Randomly arrange pennies in the spaces around the animals. In the quilt shown, some large pennies have small pennies in their centers; others do not. Save three small pennies for the letter border, or cut extras if needed. Check your composition. When you are happy with the placement of all of the animals and pennies, fuse everything in place. Be sure to follow the manufacturer's instructions.

4. Blanket stitch each piece in place. With fabric markers or embroidery stitches, add details such as eyes, ears, tails, or stripes. Refer to "Stitching" on page 14 as needed.

5. Arrange the letters around the outer edges. Separate each phrase with a small penny. Check placement, fuse, and appliqué the letters by using the blanket stitch.

6. Prepare the pieces for the cotton tongue border, referring to "Tongue Borders" on page 54. If you are making the quilt in wool or felt, blanket stitch around the rounded edges of the wool or felt tongues. This is not necessary with the cotton pieces.

7. Arrange the tongues, right side down, around the quilt edges. Center 19 tongues on each long edge and 13 tongues on each short edge. Leave ⅜" at each corner. The tongues will temporarily overlap at the corners. Baste in place.

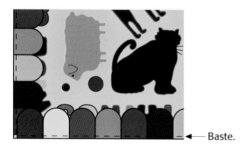

← Baste.

8. Sew the longer red border strips to the top and bottom, and then sew the shorter red strips to the sides.

Add the top and bottom borders.

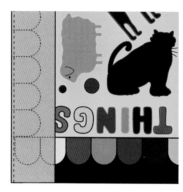

Add the side borders.

9. Layer the quilt top with the batting and backing. Pin or baste the layers together. Quilt around each animal and around the tops of the tongue border.

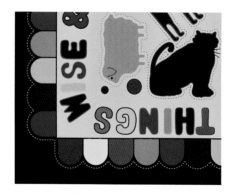

10. Trim the backing and batting even with the quilt top. Bind the quilt with the 1½"-wide yellow strips.

11. Sign and date your quilt.

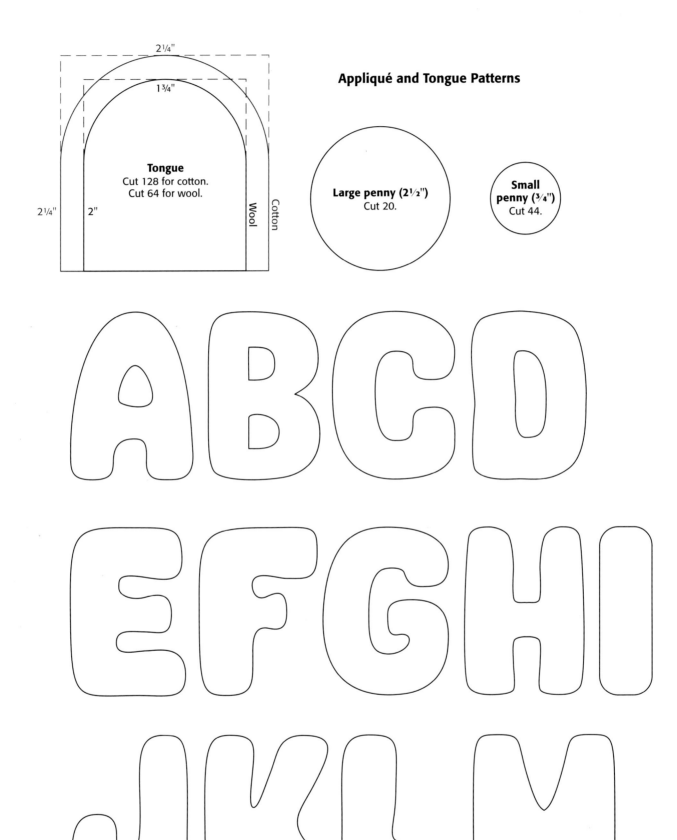

Appliqué and Tongue Patterns

2¼"

1¾"

Tongue
Cut 128 for cotton.
Cut 64 for wool.

2¼" 2" Wool Cotton

Large penny (2½")
Cut 20.

Small penny (¾")
Cut 44.

Embroider
details.

Sheep

Appliqué Patterns

Embroider
details.

Appliqué Patterns

Dog

Embroider
details.

Owl

Embroider details.

Tiger

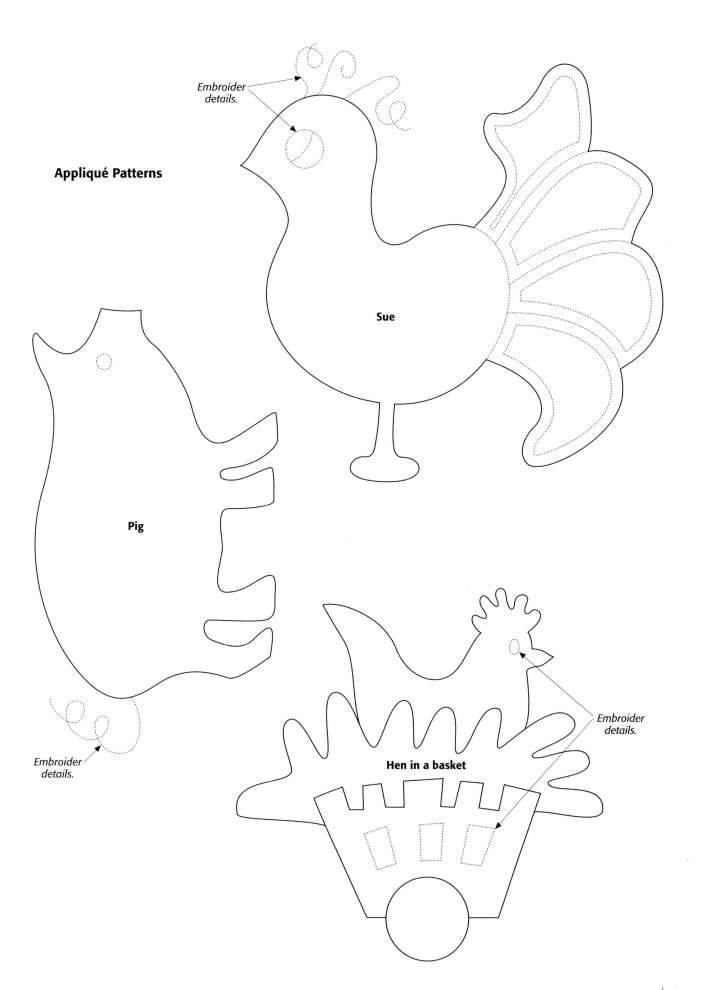

Appliqué Patterns

Embroider details.

Sue

Pig

Embroider details.

Embroider details.

Hen in a basket

Appliqué Patterns

Embroider details.

Lion

Embroider details.

Giraffe

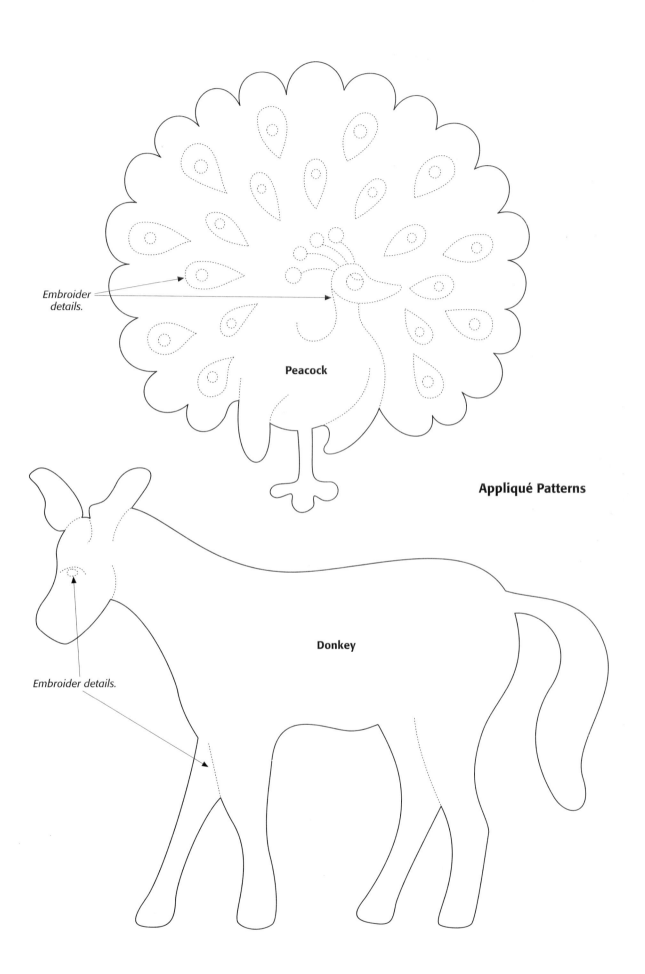

Embroider details.

Peacock

Appliqué Patterns

Donkey

Embroider details.

Appliqué Patterns

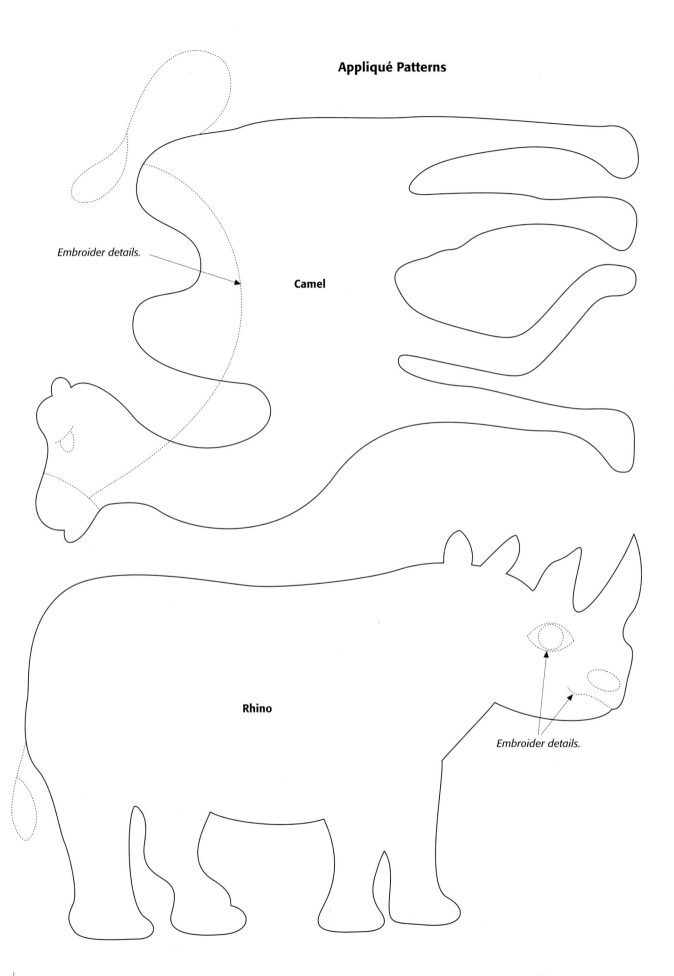

Embroider details.

Camel

Rhino

Embroider details.

Appliqué Patterns

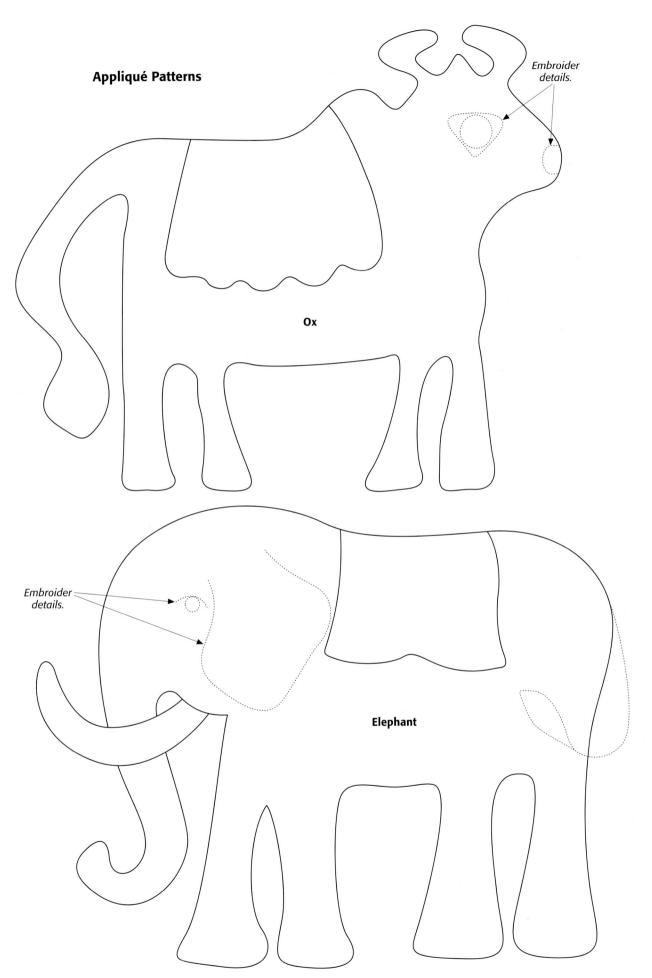

Embroider
details.

Ox

Embroider
details.

Elephant

Appliqué Patterns

Rooster

Embroider
detail.

Embroider
detail.

Goose

Rita

Embroider
details.

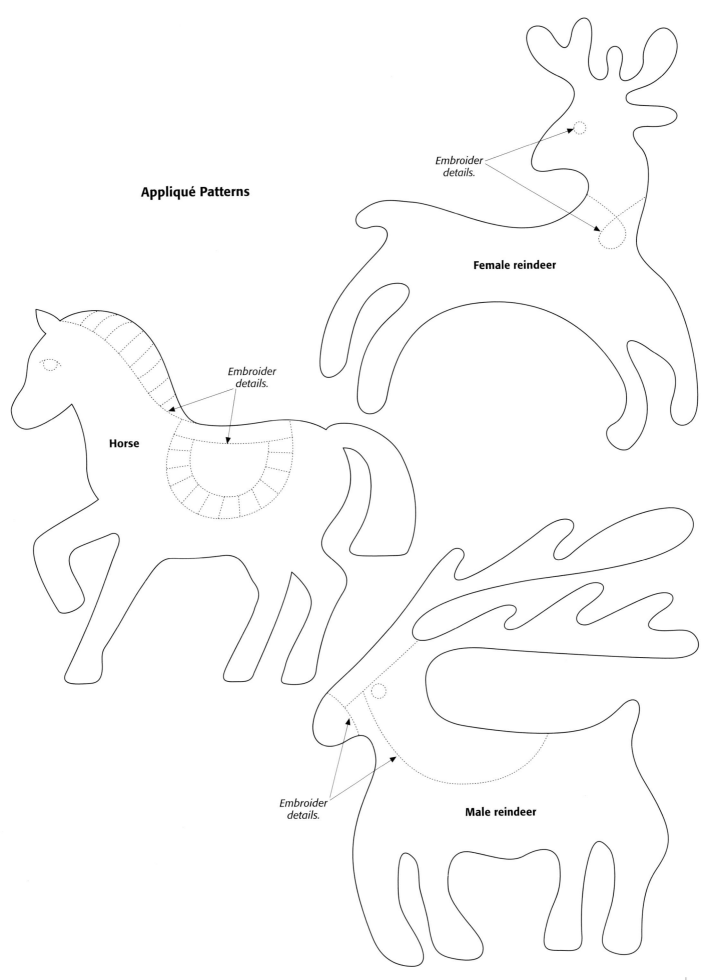

Appliqué Patterns

Embroider details.

Female reindeer

Embroider details.

Horse

Embroider details.

Male reindeer

Appliqué Patterns

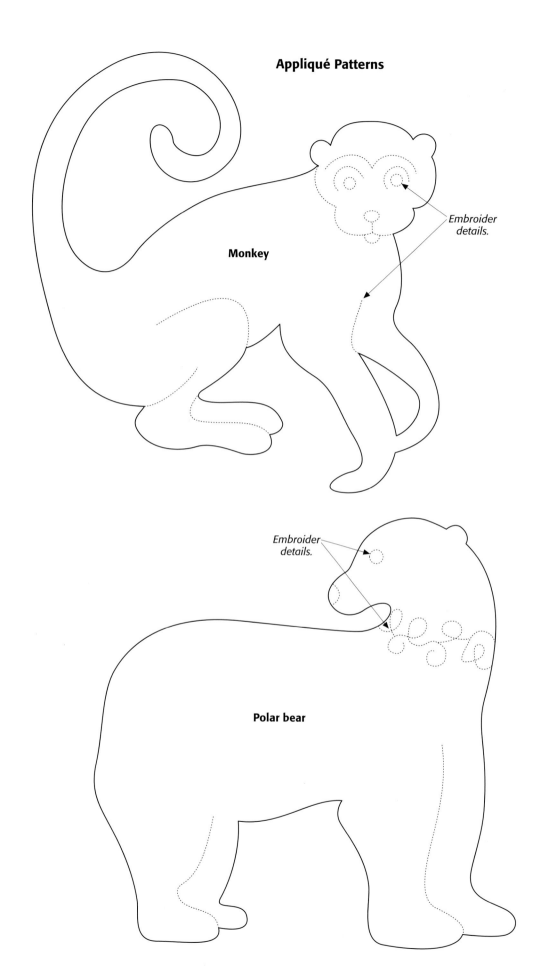

Monkey

Embroider details.

Embroider details.

Polar bear

Appliqué Patterns

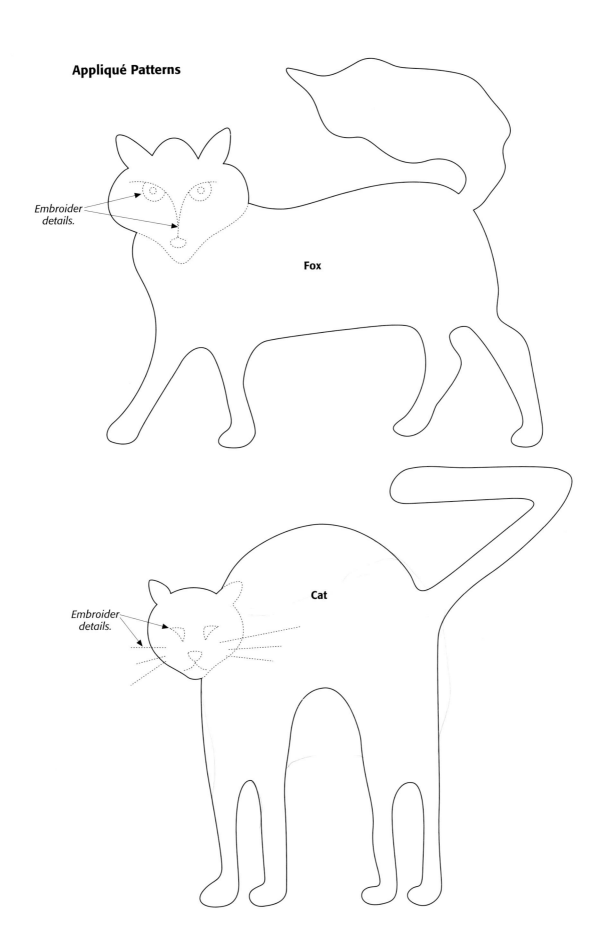

Embroider
details.

Fox

Cat

Embroider
details.

LANTERNS IN THE NIGHT

Finished size: 31½" x 25"

From the collection of Milton and Sue Ellen Chwasky

Color is a very effective way to set a mood. For "Lanterns in the Night," dark, subdued colors help establish a nighttime mood, with paper lanterns casting a soft glow on the jungle animals partying into the night. This fun penny rug can be made in any fabric. The example shown and instructions given are for wool and felt.

MATERIALS

Dimensions given are for prewashed wool.

- 25" x 31½" piece of navy blue wool for background
- 22" x 28" piece of dark brown wool for elephant, trees, pennies, and tongues*
- 12" x 18" piece of dark green wool for camel, pennies, leaves, and tongues*
- 12" x 18" piece of medium green wool for monkey, pennies, leaves, and tongues*
- 12" x 18" piece of medium brown wool for giraffe, pennies, leaves, and tongues*
- 12" x 18" piece of light brown wool for tiger, pennies, leaves, and tongues*
- 12" x 18" piece of dark gold wool for lion, pennies, leaves, and tongues*
- 6" x 8" piece of gold wool for lantern pennies
- 4" x 6" piece of white wool for lanterns
- ⅞ yard of cotton fabric for backing
- 1 fat quarter of cotton fabric for binding
- Gold and green embroidery floss
- Narrow ribbon or string

*If you prefer to use cotton, purchase extra fabric for the tongues.

CUTTING

Using the patterns on pages 64, 66, 68, 69, 72, and 77, make templates and prepare the wool pieces for appliqué. See "Trans-ferring Patterns" on pages 13 and "Cutting Circles" on page 53 for additional details.

From the wool fabrics, cut:

- 1 camel from dark green
- 1 monkey from medium green
- 1 elephant from dark brown
- 2 of tree trunk #1 from dark brown
- 2 of tree trunk #2 from dark brown
- 1 giraffe from medium brown
- 1 tiger from light brown
- 1 lion from dark gold
- 5 lanterns from white
- 5 large pennies from gold

From the remaining scraps, cut:

- 32 large pennies
- 52 small pennies
- 35 palm leaves in assorted 2" and 2½" sizes
- 54 tongues*, 1¾" x 2"

From the fat quarter, cut:

- 7 strips, 1½" x 21" (or bias strips to total 124" for binding)

* Round the corners of the tongues, or make a template with the pattern on page 77.

ASSEMBLY

1. Blanket stitch a white lantern to each gold penny. Refer to "Stitching" on page 14.

2. Assemble 32 penny stacks by securing one small penny to the center of each large penny with a blanket stitch.

3. Arrange all of the appliqué pieces and tongues on the navy blue background fabric, referring to the photo at left for placement.

4. When you are satisfied with the arrangement, pin or baste the pieces in place. Blanket stitch each piece to the background fabric.

5. To help visualize the "ropes" that the lanterns and monkey are suspended from, pin a piece of narrow ribbon or string to the background where you will chain stitch the ropes.

6. Add chain-stitched details to the animals and tree trunks; use the markings on the patterns as a guide. Replace the ribbon or string ropes with chain stitches.

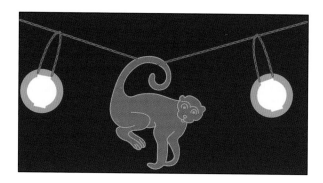

7. Echo quilt around each lantern penny; use two strands of gold embroidery floss to make them "glow."

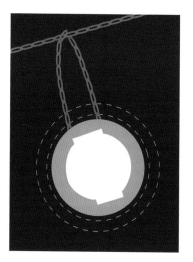

8. Add backing fabric and bind the penny rug as you would a quilt with the 1½" binding strips. Refer to "Finishing the Project" on pages 17–21.

THE LAST DETAIL

Use a stripe or plaid fabric for the binding and cut it on the bias as I did to add one last bit of fun to the animals' late-night party.

9. Sign and date your penny rug.

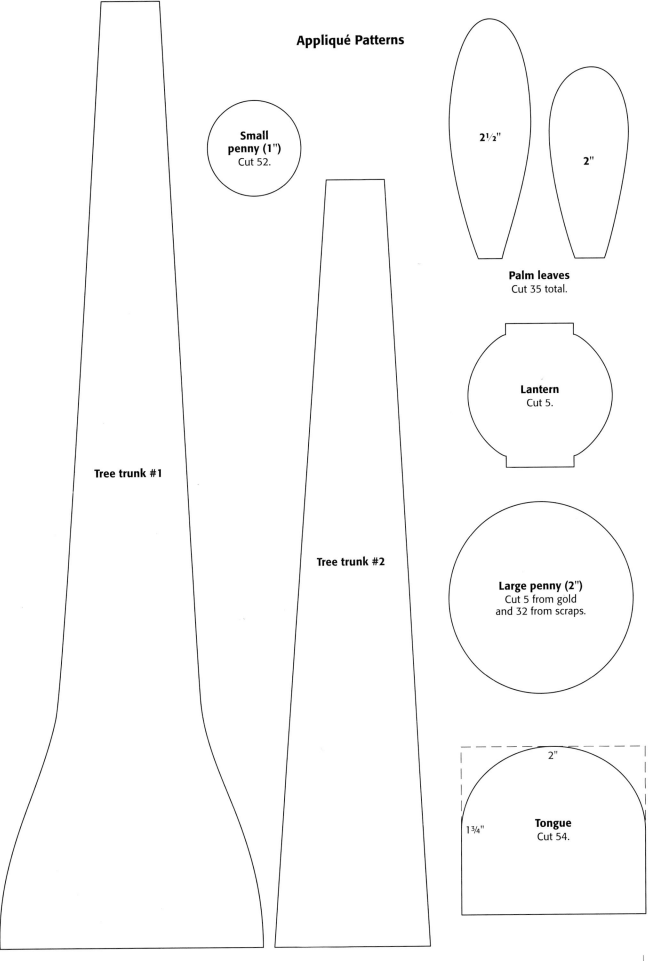

Appliqué Patterns

Small penny (1")
Cut 52.

2½"

2"

Palm leaves
Cut 35 total.

Lantern
Cut 5.

Tree trunk #1

Tree trunk #2

Large penny (2")
Cut 5 from gold
and 32 from scraps.

2"

1¾"

Tongue
Cut 54.

HARVEST WALTZ

Finished size: 60" x 18"

I originally designed this merry harvest scene as a rug-hooking pattern. It never got hooked, but now I can finally enjoy my motley crew of moonlighters whenever I like. The runner is made from cotton, and the following directions use the mini-fuse appliqué technique on page 16. The design is equally effective in wool or felt. Be creative and select your own colors for the appliqué pieces.

MATERIALS

Yardage is based on 42"-wide cotton fabric.

- 1¼ yards of dark blue solid for background
- ½ yard of medium blue solid for background of tongue border
- 10 fat quarters of assorted solids for appliqué pieces and tongues
- 1¼ yards of fabric for pieced backing (or 1⅞ yards for unpieced backing)
- Lightweight fusible web (for cotton only)
- Embroidery floss to match appliqué pieces

CUTTING

Use the patterns on pages 82–91. Before cutting and preparing any of the cotton appliqué pieces, read "Mini-Fuse Cotton Appliqué" on page 16. Trace the patterns onto fusible web and fuse the pieces to the wrong side of the fabric before cutting. Remember to trace the patterns backward when you are using the mini-fuse appliqué technique.

From the dark blue solid, cut:
- 1 piece, 18½" x 40½"

From the assorted solids, cut out and prepare the appliqué pieces.

From the remaining assorted solids, cut:
- 172 tongues*, 2½" x 3½"

From the medium blue solid, cut:
- 10 pieces, 2½" x 18½"

From the backing fabric, cut:
- 2 pieces, 18½" x 42"

OR

- 1 piece, 18½" x 60½"

*Round off the corners freehand or use the pattern on page 82.

ASSEMBLY

1. Arrange all the pieces on the dark blue background, referring to the photo above. Take your time and make sure the composition is just what you want. When you are pleased with the arrangement, fuse. Be sure to follow the manufacturer's instructions.

2. Using matching embroidery floss, outline each piece with blanket stitches. Embroider the details, following the guides on the patterns for placement.

3. Add a horizon by drawing a straight line across the background. Be sure to leave room for the moon. (My horizon runs across the figures at about shoulder height.) Stem stitch over this line.

4. Using the pattern on page 88, make a template for the moon and add the moon outline in the same manner. To create the illusion of a rising or setting moon, draw only part of the moon showing above the horizon.

5. Randomly pair up the assorted tongue pieces. You should have a total of 86 pairs. Stitch and turn them right side out, referring to "Tongue Borders" on page 54. Blanket-stitch the long curved edge of each.

6. To make the tongue border, first lay a medium blue border strip, right side up, on your work surface. Place nine tongues on it as shown. Have raw edges even and leave ¼" of the blue showing at each end. Baste. Repeat to make a total of six strips.

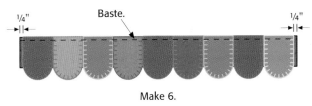

Make 6.

7. Baste eight tongues to one of the remaining blue border strips in the same manner, leaving 1¼" showing at each end. Repeat to make a total of four strips.

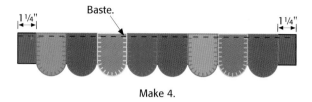

Baste.

1¼"   1¼"

Make 4.

8. Place a row of nine tongues from step 6 on one end of the background fabric with right sides together, raw edges even, and the rounded ends of the tongues pointing toward the appliqué. Stitch. Press the seam allowances toward the runner.

9. Add a row with eight tongues from step 7. Sew the rows together with tongue sides facing and edges aligned. As you add each row, move the tongues from the previous row out of the way so that they don't get caught in the seam. Add three more rows, alternating nine, eight, and nine tongues to finish one end.

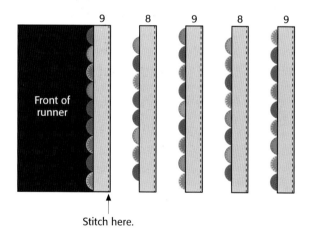

Front of runner

9   8   9   8   9

Stitch here.

10. Repeat steps 8 and 9 on the other end of the runner.

11. If you are piecing the backing, join the two 18½" x 42" pieces end to end; use a ¼"-wide seam allowance. Press the seam open and trim to 18½" x 60½".

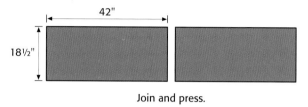

42"

18½"

Join and press.

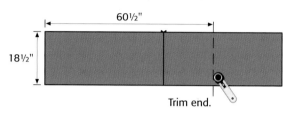

60½"

18½"

Trim end.

12. With right sides together, stitch the backing fabric to the background fabric by using a ¼"-wide seam allowance; be careful not to catch any tongues in the seam. Leave a small opening at one end of the runner. Turn the runner right side out through the opening. Slip-stitch the opening closed. Press.

13. Sign and date your table runner.

DESIGN OPTIONS

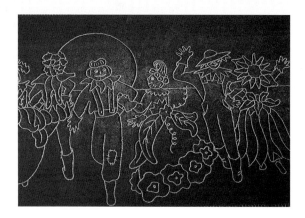

The design from "Harvest Waltz" is easily translated to embroidery, as shown here.

Surround one pair of figures with several rounds of tongues.

For a smaller design, consider working with fewer figures, perhaps two at each end.

Appliqué Patterns

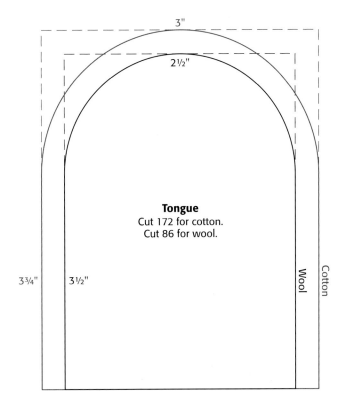

Tongue
Cut 172 for cotton.
Cut 86 for wool.

3" 2½"

3¾" 3½" Wool Cotton

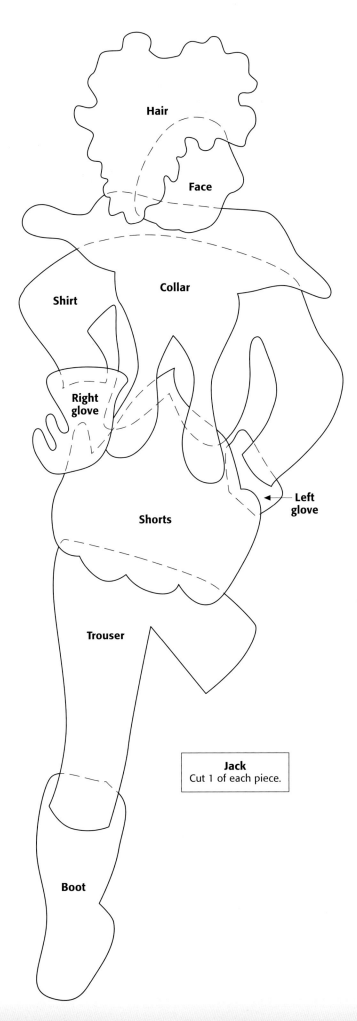

Hair

Face

Collar

Shirt

Right glove

Left glove

Shorts

Trouser

Jack
Cut 1 of each piece.

Boot

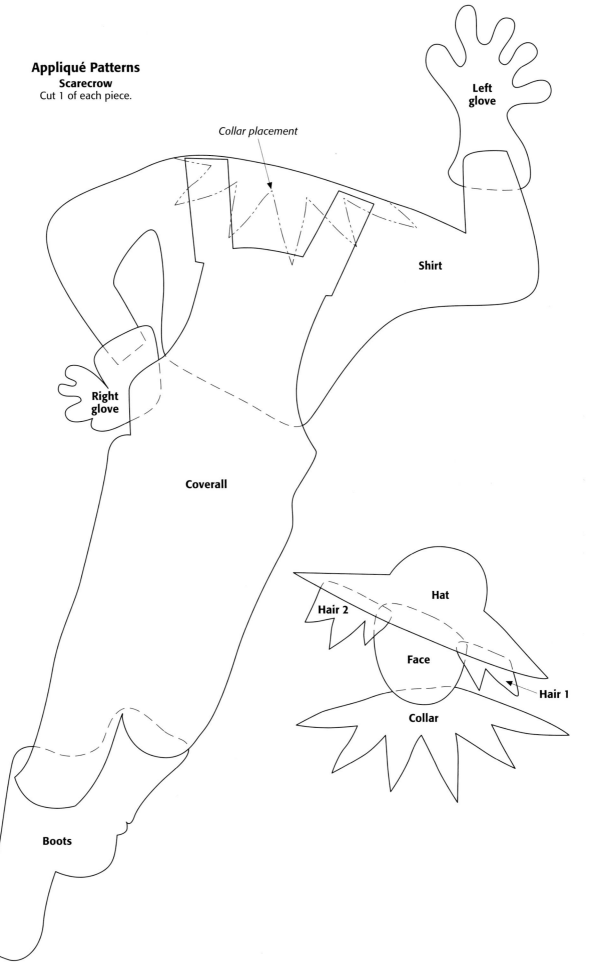

Appliqué Patterns
Scarecrow
Cut 1 of each piece.

Left glove

Collar placement

Shirt

Right glove

Coverall

Hat

Hair 2

Face

Hair 1

Collar

Boots

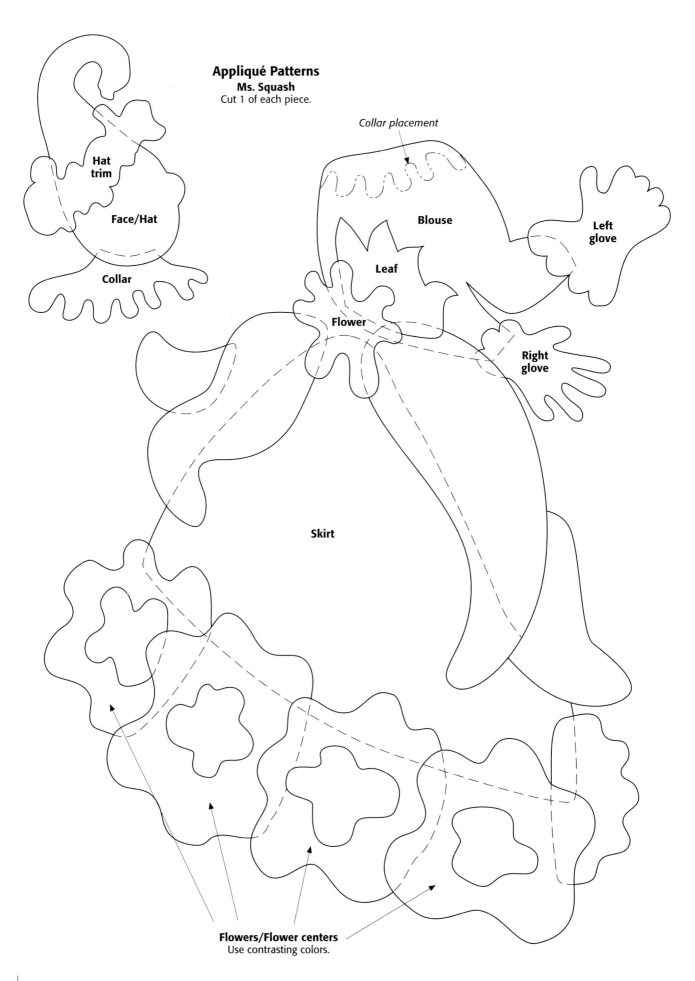

Appliqué Patterns
Ms. Squash
Cut 1 of each piece.

Hat trim

Face/Hat

Collar

Collar placement

Blouse

Left glove

Leaf

Flower

Right glove

Skirt

Flowers/Flower centers
Use contrasting colors.

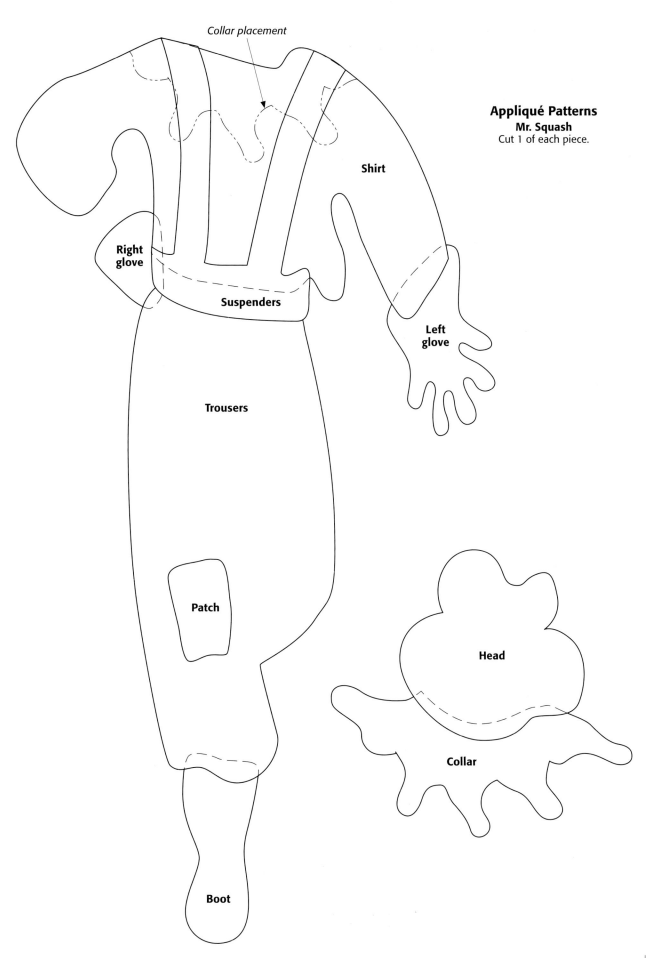

Collar placement

Appliqué Patterns
Mr. Squash
Cut 1 of each piece.

Shirt

Right glove

Suspenders

Left glove

Trousers

Patch

Head

Boot

Collar

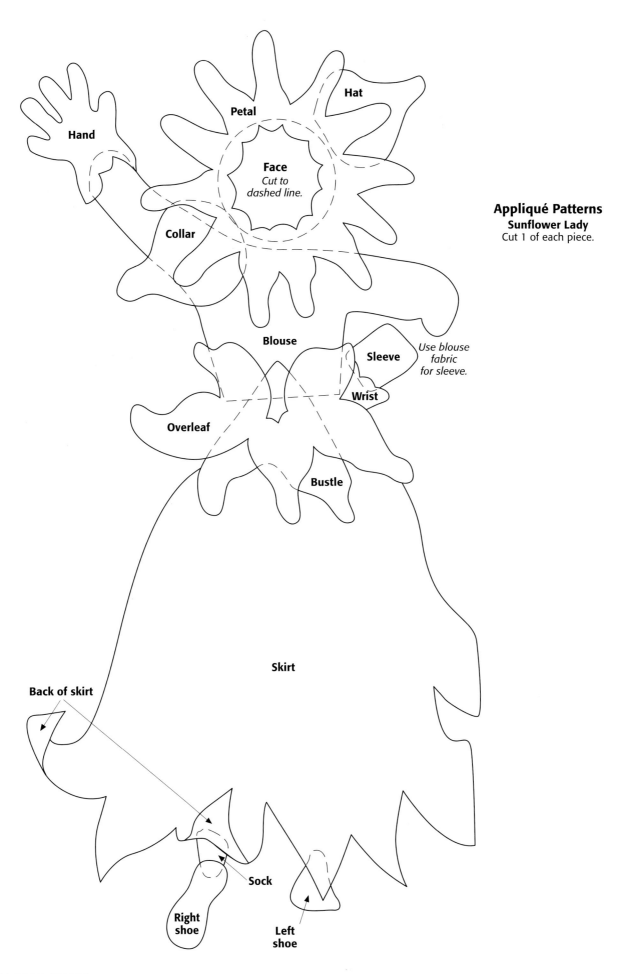

Hand

Petal

Hat

Face
Cut to dashed line.

Collar

Appliqué Patterns
Sunflower Lady
Cut 1 of each piece.

Blouse

Sleeve

Use blouse fabric for sleeve.

Wrist

Overleaf

Bustle

Skirt

Back of skirt

Sock

Right shoe

Left shoe

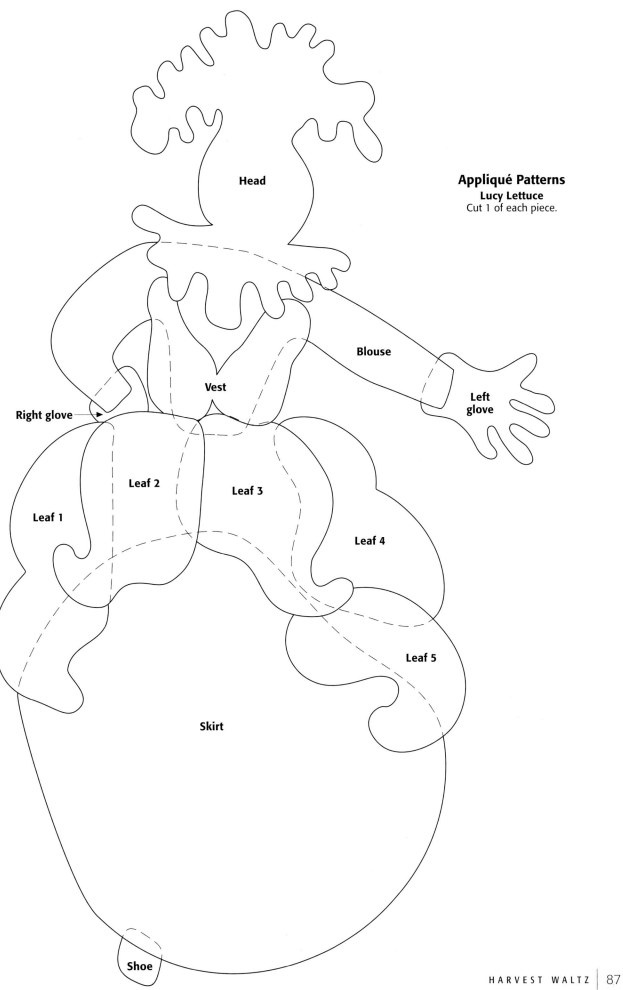

Appliqué Patterns
Lucy Lettuce
Cut 1 of each piece.

Head

Blouse

Vest

Left
glove

Right glove →

Leaf 2

Leaf 3

Leaf 1

Leaf 4

Leaf 5

Skirt

Shoe

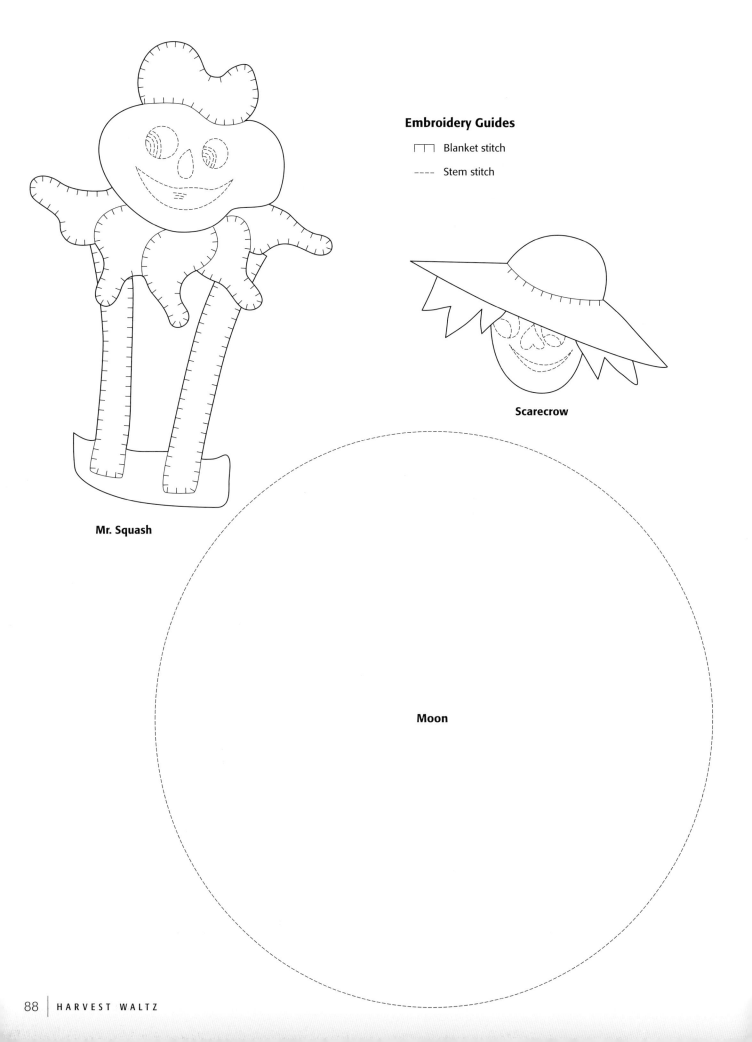

Embroidery Guides

⊓⊓ Blanket stitch

--- Stem stitch

Scarecrow

Mr. Squash

Moon

Embroidery Guide
Sunflower Lady

⊓⊓ Blanket stitch

◯◯◯ Chain stitch

∘ French knot

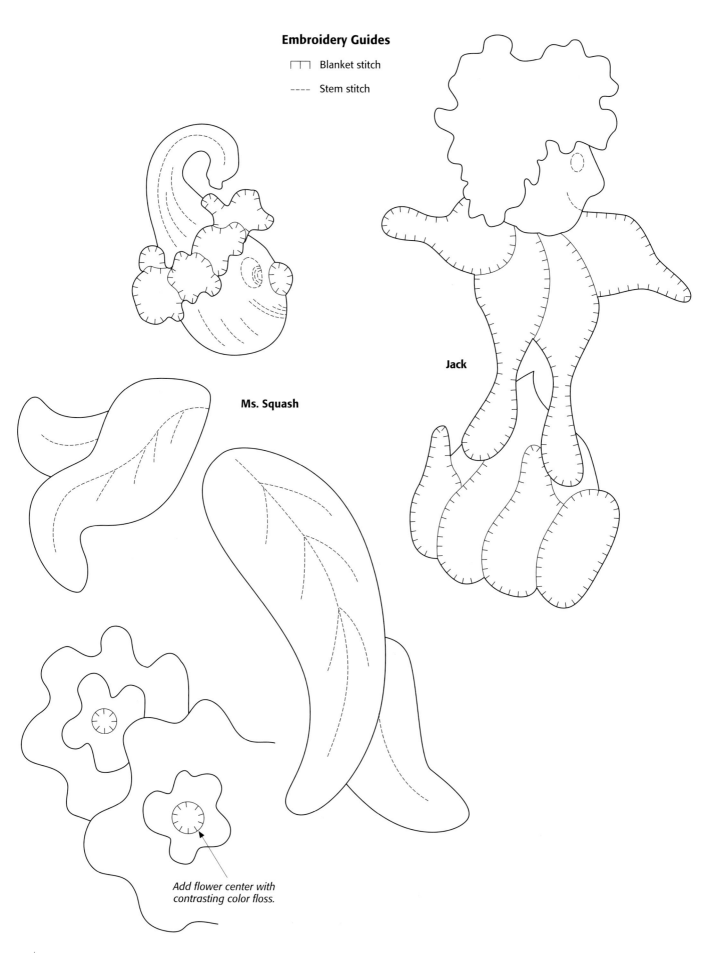

Embroidery Guides

Blanket stitch

Stem stitch

Jack

Ms. Squash

Add flower center with contrasting color floss.

Embroidery Guides
Lucy Lettuce

---- Stem stitch

PETAL HEARTS

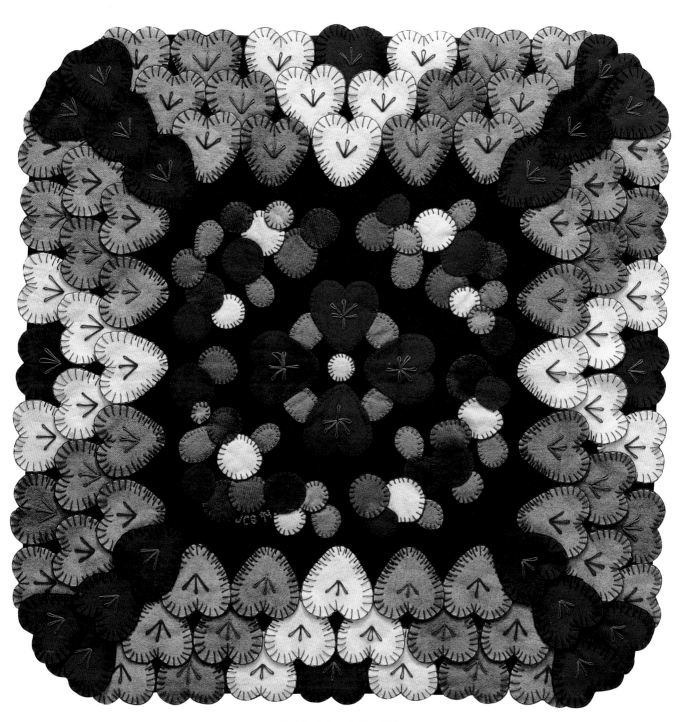

Finished size: 32" x 32"

I love the texture and dimension you get in petal rugs. The hearts are ideal take-along projects; you can do the hand stitching while traveling or waiting for appointments. For this petal rug, I added a batting layer and quilted it, making a warm and cozy lap robe, table topper, or wall hanging.

MATERIALS

Dimensions given are for prewashed wool.

- 1 yard of black wool for background (32" x 32" piece)
- 16" x 24" piece *each* of cream, green, tan, and cranberry wool for hearts
- 10" x 10" piece *each* of cream, green, tan, brown, rose, and cranberry wool for flowers and leaves
- 1⅛ yards of cotton fabric for backing
- ½ yard of cotton fabric for bias binding
- 34" x 34" piece of lightweight batting
- Perle cotton (#8) or embroidery floss in coordinating or contrasting colors

CUTTING

From the black wool, cut:

1 piece, 32" x 32"

Using the patterns on page 96, make templates for the appliqué pieces. Referring to the cutting chart below, trace the templates and prepare the pieces for appliqué. See "Transferring Patterns" on page 13 for additional details. I cut each small, medium, and large flower a slightly different size to add to the folksy charm of the design.

Pattern Piece	Color and Number to Cut					
	Cream	Green	Tan	Brown	Rose	Cranberry
Hearts	20	24	24	–	–	24
Large Flowers	5	–	5	1	3	5
Medium Flowers	3	–	4	8	6	–
Small Flowers	1	–	1	–	–	–
Leaves	–	15	–	–	–	–

ASSEMBLY

1. Using one strand of perle cotton, work the blanket stitch around all of the hearts except the four cranberry hearts that go in the center of the quilt. See "Stitching" on page 14. As you work, leave space between the stitches for a second row of stitches that you'll use to attach the heart to the background. See step 6 on page 95. Begin and end the row of blanket stitches at the point of the heart so that no knots show on the floppy top "petals" of the heart pieces.

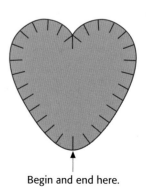

Begin and end here.

2. With chalk, pins, or basting thread, mark the center lines on the black background. Then measure and mark 7½" in from the outer edge along each line and place the point of one cream heart at each of these marks.

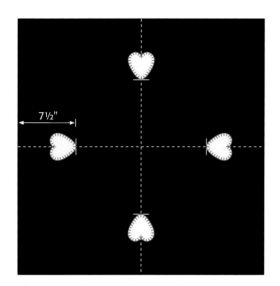

3. Working from the center cream heart toward the corners, add the other hearts in the first row. Use a ruler or yardstick to check the straightness of the row and to check the distances between hearts as you place them. Place the hearts so that they just touch at their widest point. Each corner heart overlaps the hearts on its sides. Pin each heart in the first row with just one pin near the point.

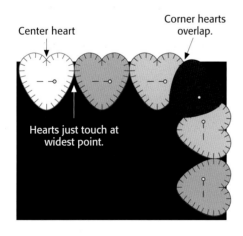

Center heart

Corner hearts overlap.

Hearts just touch at widest point.

THREAD ADVICE

Try to cut the perle cotton long enough to go all the way around a heart without having to change thread. For me, about 40" was just right, but the size and closeness of your stitches will determine what is right for you.

4. Referring to the illustration for color placement, pin the second row of hearts so that the point of each heart lies under the first row at the point where two hearts touch. Repeat for the third row. It's okay if the tops of the hearts in the third row hang over the edge of the background.

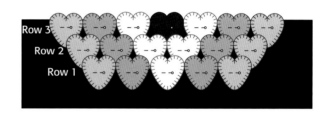

Row 3

Row 2

Row 1

PIN POINTER

This is one time I do not recommend using sequin pins. You may be doing quite a bit of adjusting as you work, and longer straight pins are easier to grab and move.

5. At the outer corner, overlap two hearts of the same color as shown.

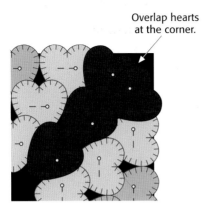

Overlap hearts at the corner.

NOTE: *Be prepared to play around with the placement of the hearts. The design isn't exact, which of course is the charm of all folk art.*

6. Using the blanket stitch, appliqué the hearts to the background. Work the new stitches between the first set of stitches, attaching only the bottom half of the heart to the background. Pin back the tops of the overlapping hearts as you work.

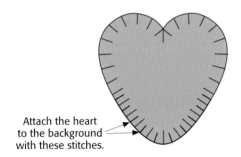

Attach the heart to the background with these stitches.

7. With contrasting perle cotton, work large lazy daisy stitches in all of the hearts as shown. See "Stitching" on page 14.

8. Arrange the center hearts, flowers, and leaves, following the diagram below or choosing your own pleasing arrangement. When you are satisfied with the design, pin the pieces in place. Then appliqué the pieces by using the blanket stitch.

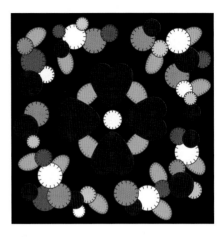

9. Embroider the center hearts with a lazy daisy stitch as shown.

10. Using the embroidery stitches of your choice, initial and date the front of your petal rug. See "Labeling Your Work" on page 17.

FINISHING

Refer to "Finishing the Project" on pages 17–21 for additional details.

1. Layer the rug top with batting and backing. Pin or baste the three layers together.

2. Quilt the center area.

3. Leave the corners square or round them off by using a plate or saucer as a guide. Be sure to fold the "petals" of the hearts away from the cutting line.

4. Press the back of the rug, placing a damp cloth between the rug and the iron.

5. Bind the edges. Be sure to use bias-cut binding strips if you cut the rounded corners.

SHORTCUT

Use ½"-wide purchased double-fold bias tape for binding if you prefer.

Appliqué Patterns

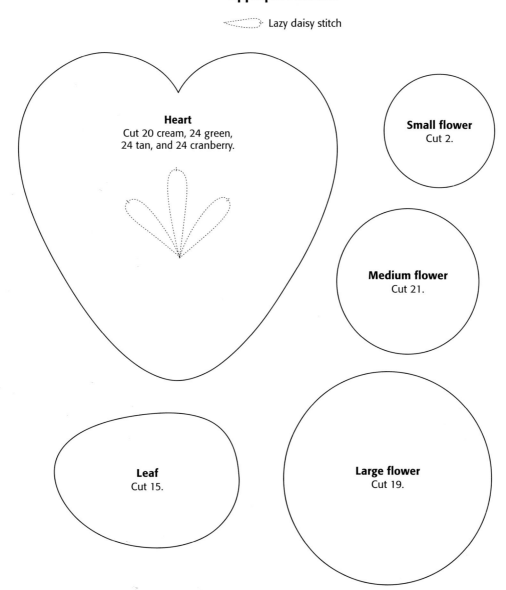

Lazy daisy stitch

Heart
Cut 20 cream, 24 green, 24 tan, and 24 cranberry.

Small flower
Cut 2.

Medium flower
Cut 21.

Leaf
Cut 15.

Large flower
Cut 19.

TRADITIONAL HOOKED RUGS ᕙᕉᕉᕉᕙ

Rug hooking, like quilting, is a recycler's dream come true. This all-American craft became popular in the mid-1800s, when burlap, the fabric most commonly used for the foundation, became more readily available. Cast-off burlap feed sacks became the framework for rugs that featured designs of the family home, its occupants, pets, and garden. Subject matter also included wild and whimsical geometric and abstract designs. Any fabric on hand might find its way into the top of the rug, including Dad's old military uniform, Aunt Edna's mourning gown, and Jimmy's red flannel long johns! Women drew their own designs or purchased patterns from peddlers passing through town.

Like so many crafts, rug hooking has passed in and out of style over the years. Happily, it enjoys an ever-growing renaissance today.

RED HEN RUG

Finished size: 24¾" x 19¾"

Little Red Hen certainly resembles women of the twenty-first century. She plants, grows, harvests, and mills the wheat. And then she bakes the cake, all while taking care of the kids too! But then, most women have always been working women. I used all recycled wools and dyed them to make this spirited rug.

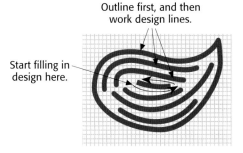

Materials

Wool yardage is based on 54"-wide prewashed wool.

- 33" x 28" piece of foundation fabric
- ¾ yard *total* of wool in assorted reds and pinks for hen, details, and border
- ⅝ yard *total* of wool in assorted purples and lavenders for background and border
- ⅜ yard *total* of wool in assorted greens for vegetation and background
- ⅜ yard *total* of wool in assorted yellows and ochres for chicks, wheat, hen's feet, and other details
- ¼ yard *total* of wool in assorted blues for chicken coop and sky
- 15" x 20" *total* of wool in assorted browns and tans for background and details
- #5 cutting head
- Permanent marker to transfer design
- 3 yards of rug tape or twill tape for finishing

Hooking the Rug

1. Cut the wool into ⁵⁄₃₂"-wide strips (#5 cut), referring to "Cutting Strips" on page 25.

2. Enlarge and trace the pattern (page 101) onto the foundation fabric, referring to "Preparing the Foundation" on page 26.

3. Start by hooking the outer edge of Red Hen's wing. Then fill in the area with rows, following the direction of the arrows and changing colors as desired. Following the contours of the wing

gives the hen a more three-dimensional quality. Refer to "Hooking" on page 27 for additional details as needed.

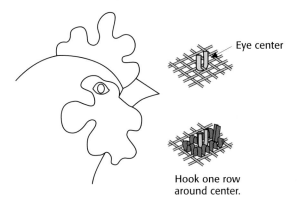

4. Hook the center of the eye by pulling up one end of the wool in one hole and pulling up the other end in the next hole. Leave the ends of the wool long for now. Hook the circle around the center of the eye.

5. Hook the beak. Hook one row of background around the edge. Hook the brown area around the eye, the comb, the part that I unscientifically call the "gobble-gobble" part of the head, and the head feathers. Now you can clip the eye center's tail ends even with the tops of the wool loops (and clip any other strip ends enclosed by stitches).

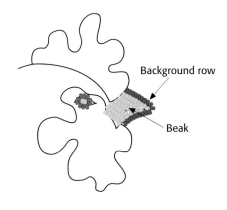

6. Continue hooking, outlining design areas and filling them in. Refer to the color key on the pattern and the color photo on page 98.

7. **Henhouse:** Using straight-line hooking and following the lines of the siding on the henhouse pattern, hook in straight, horizontal rows. I hooked two rows of bright blue, one row of dark blue, two rows of bright, and one of dark, continuing from the top to the bottom. Depending upon your hooking style, the lines of wool loops may or may not match up with the drawn lines. (Mine did not!) But the end effect is all that matters.

8. **Background:** I like to use many shades of one color when I hook the background areas. I pick up the colors randomly from my basket and follow the contours of the design, filling in around it. Wavy directional hooking is more interesting to look at even if you use just one solid color for your background.

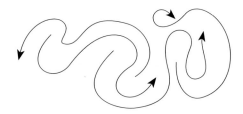

Hook in wavy lines.

9. **Border:** With a permanent marker, write your initials and the year somewhere in the border. Hook the letters, numbers, and the grains of wheat; then, with straight lines, fill in around them with your border color. Hook the border in sections, hooking the details first and then filling in with straight rows.

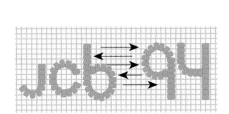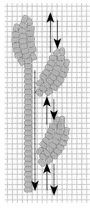

Fill in straight lines.

TURNING CORNERS

Draw a diagonal line at each corner and use the lines as a guide for changing direction.

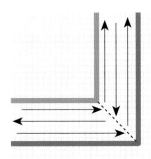

Change direction at the dotted line.

10. After the hooking is completed, refer to "Finishing the Rug" on page 29.

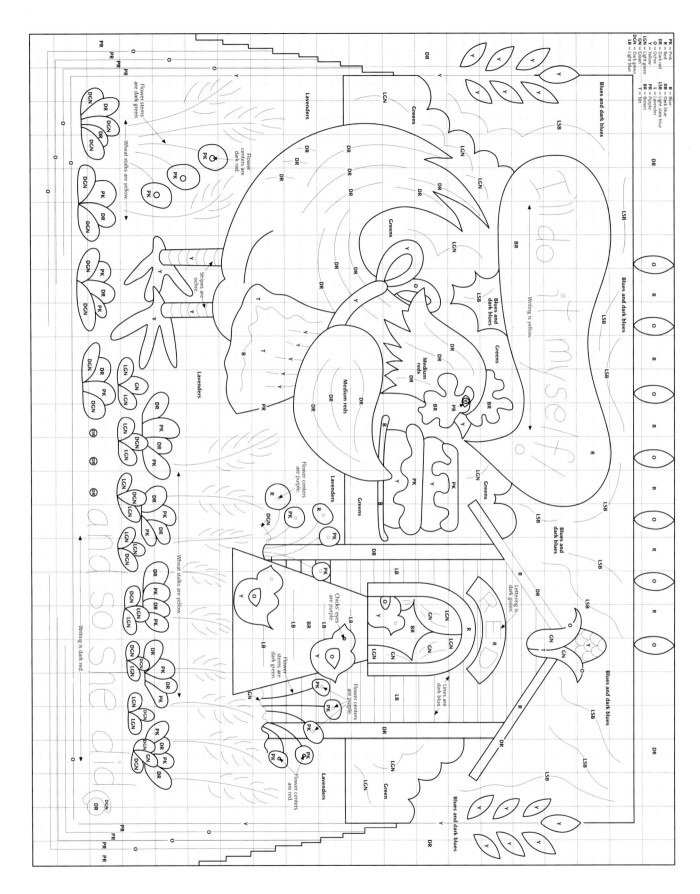

Red Hen Rug
One square equals ½".
Enlarge pattern 200% and then 143% (286% total)
to 24¾" x 19¾".

RED RUNNING HORSE

Finished size: 12" x 7"

A starry night and a running horse; what could be better? This little rug could be worked in any color scheme, for any room in your home. The small size makes it a good beginner project or a wonderful gift for anyone who appreciates folk-art designs, fabrics, and textiles.

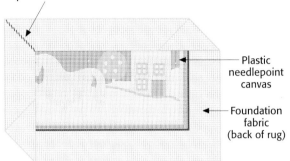

MATERIALS

Wool yardage is based on 54"-wide prewashed wool.

- 20" x 15" piece of foundation fabric
- ¼ yard of navy wool for background, border, and door
- ¼ yard of red wool for horse, tree trunk, house, chimney, and border
- ¼ yard of gold wool for ground, roof, windows, apples, and stars
- 4" x 12" piece of green wool for tree, sidewalk, and house details
- 1 fat quarter of cotton fabric for backing
- 10½" x 13½" piece of plastic needlepoint canvas*
- #4 cutting head
- Permanent marker to transfer design

This canvas helps to stabilize the rug for use as a wall hanging.

HOOKING THE RUG

1. Cut the wool into ⅛"-wide strips (#4 cut), referring to "Cutting Strips" on page 25.

2. Enlarge and trace the pattern (page 104) onto the foundation fabric by using a permanent marker and a light box. Refer to "Preparing the Foundation" on page 26.

3. Hook the design by using the photograph as a guide. Refer to "Hooking" on page 27 for additional details as needed.

4. Trim the foundation fabric down to a 2" border all around the hooked area. Cut the plastic needlepoint canvas just slightly smaller than the hooked area. Set the needlepoint canvas on the back of the rug. Miter the corners of the foundation fabric, enclosing the needlepoint canvas on the back. Stitch just the corners.

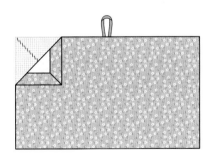

Slip-stitch corners.

Plastic needlepoint canvas

Foundation fabric (back of rug)

5. Cut the cotton fabric about 2" larger than the rug. Fold the edges of the cotton fabric under to fit the back of the rug and slip-stitch the cotton to the back of the rug. Add a ribbon loop to the top center in back for hanging your hooked rug. The plastic canvas will keep the corners of the rug from drooping down when it is hung.

Red Running Horse Rug
One square equals ½".
Enlarge pattern 125%
to 12" x 7".

KITTY

Finished size (including tongue border): 14½" x 12"

It's hard to resist a cute little kitten with prancing white paws. This small but charming hooked rug is framed with a floppy tongue border. Of course, if you have a cat, you know that your own kitty will think you made this just for him or her!

MATERIALS

Wool yardage is based on 54"-wide prewashed wool.

- 18" x 16" piece of foundation fabric
- ¼ yard of gold wool for flowers, letters, border, and tongues
- ¼ yard of green wool for vine, leaves, and tongues
- ¼ yard of light reddish brown wool for background
- ¼ yard of rose wool for flowers and border
- 10" x 12" piece of black wool for cat
- 8" x 12" piece of white wool for cat
- 1 fat quarter of cotton fabric for backing
- #4 cutting head
- Embroidery floss
- Permanent marker to transfer design

Hooking the Rug

1. Cut the wool into ⅛"-wide strips (#4 cut), referring to "Cutting Strips" on page 25.

2. Cut out 16 gold tongues and 16 green tongues by using the patterns below.

3. Enlarge and trace the pattern (page 107) onto the foundation fabric with a permanent marker and a light box. Refer to "Preparing the Foundation" on page 26.

4. Hook the design by using the photograph as a guide. Refer to "Hooking" on page 27 for additional details as needed.

5. Trim the foundation fabric down to a 2" border all around the hooked rug. Hand sew a line of running stitches along the outer edge of the foundation fabric. Pull it up to gather the excess fabric.

6. Using two strands of embroidery floss, blanket stitch the curved edge of each tongue. Arrange the smaller green tongues around the border. Slip-stitch the tongues in place to the back of the rug.

7. Arrange the larger gold tongues behind the green tongues. Slip-stitch these tongues in place.

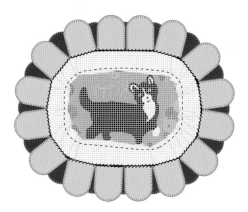

8. Cut the cotton fabric about 2" larger than the hooked part of the rug. Fold the edges of the cotton fabric to fit the back of the rug and slip-stitch the cotton in place, covering the stitched edges of the tongues at the same time.

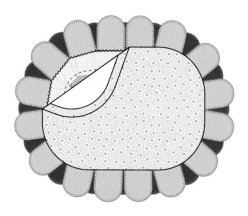

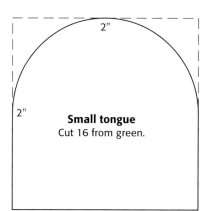

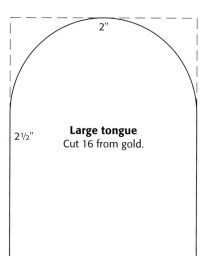

2"

2"

2"

2½"

Small tongue
Cut 16 from green.

Large tongue
Cut 16 from gold.

Kitty Rug
One square equals ½".
Enlarge pattern 125%
to 10½" x 7¾".

40 DAYS AND 40 NIGHTS

Finished size: 14½" x 9"

Here's another wonderful way to depict and pay tribute to Noah's long, wet ordeal. The background of the cloudy day is gray and the night is black, but the bright and cheerful animals make this a fun project to hook, and it will be a bright addition to any room in your home.

MATERIALS

Wool yardage is based on 54"-wide prewashed wool.
- 22" x 18" piece of foundation fabric
- ¼ yard of black wool for eyes and background
- ¼ yard of gray wool for background
- ¼ yard of red wool for deer, boat, border, and details
- 10" x 20" piece of yellow wool for giraffes and letters
- 10" x 18" piece of orange wool for elephants and boat details
- 10" x 12" piece of pink wool for kangaroos
- 10" x 12" piece of green wool for rhinos
- 1 fat quarter of cotton fabric for backing
- 13⅝" x 22⅝" piece of plastic needlepoint canvas* (or 1 piece at least 10" x 15")
- #4 cutting head
- Permanent marker to transfer design

This canvas helps to stabilize the rug for use as a wall hanging.

HOOKING THE RUG

1. Cut the wool into ⅛"-wide strips (#4 cut), referring to "Cutting Strips" on page 25.

2. Enlarge and trace the pattern (page 110) onto the foundation fabric with a permanent marker and a light box. Refer to "Preparing the Foundation" on page 26.

3. Hook the design by using the photograph as a guide. Refer to "Hooking" on page 27 for additional details as needed.

4. Trim the foundation fabric down to a 2" border all around the hooked rug. Cut the plastic needlepoint canvas just slightly smaller than the hooked area. Set the needlepoint canvas on the back of the rug. Miter the bottom corners and gently gather the top curve of the foundation fabric, enclosing the needlepoint canvas on the back. Use a basting stitch along the curve if needed. Stitch just the corners.

5. Cut the cotton fabric about 2" larger than the rug. Fold the edges of the cotton fabric to fit the back of the rug and slip-stitch the cotton to the rug. Add a ribbon loop to the top center in back for hanging your hooked rug. The plastic canvas will keep the rug stable when it is hung.

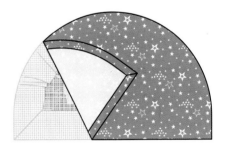

**40 Days and
40 Nights Rug**
One square equals ½".
Enlarge pattern 133%
to 14½" x 9".

RESOURCES AND INSPIRATION

Appleton Krafts and Supplies
50 Appleton Avenue
South Hamilton, MA 01982
1-978-468-7778
Rug-hooking frame

Association of Traditional Hooking Artists
Contact: Joan Cahill
ATHA National Membership
600½ Maple Street
Endicott, NY 13760
Email: jcahill29@aol.com
1-607-748-7588

B. Black & Sons—Kings Road Imports
548 South Los Angeles Street
Los Angeles, CA 90013
1-800-433-1546
Wool

Harry M. Fraser Co.
R&R Machine Co., Inc.
433 Duggins Road
Stoneville, NC 27048
1-336-573-9830
Cutters

Mayflower Textile
PO Box 329
Franklin, MA 02038-0329
Puritan frames

National Nonwovens
180 Pleasant Street
Easthampton, MA 01027
1-800-333-3469
Wool felt

W. Cushing and Company
PO Box 351
Kennebunkport, ME 04046-0351
1-800-626-7847
www.wcushing.com
Wool, dyeing, and rug-hooking supplies

SUGGESTED READING

The Complete Rug Hooker: A Guide to the Craft by Joan Moshimer; published by Dover Books in New York.

Folk Art Friends by Polly Minick and Laurie Simpson; published by Martingale & Company in Woodinville, Washington.

Purely Primitive by Pat Cross; published by Martingale & Company in Woodinville, Washington.

Rug Hooking Magazine
1300 Market Street, Suite 202
Lemoyne, PA 17043-9943
1-800-233-9055
For the most up-to-date and extensive information on supplies, tools, teachers, workshops, and ideas, you must check out this magazine.

Warm Up to Wool: Projects to Hook and Stitch; published by Martingale & Company in Woodinville, Washington.

ABOUT THE AUTHOR

Janet Carija Brandt lives in Indianapolis, Indiana, with her husband. She has worked with textiles in one way or another most of her life. She continues to enjoy all of the wonderful traditional skills of appliqué, embroidery, and rug hooking, while also embracing the twenty-first century and the wonders of digitized embroidery and embroidery machines. She is creating a new collection of wool appliqués that will illustrate an upcoming inspirational book. Janet also works as a designer for Husqvarna Viking, expanding the conventions of two-dimensional machine embroidery into three-dimensional dolls and miniature theaters or scenes. Most of all, Janet is tickled pink to see her first book about the joys of working with wool revised 10 years later.